The Omnipotent S

A Study in Self-Deception and Self-Cure

by

Paul Bousfield

Chapter 1. The Unconscious Mind

§1

In considering the question of character, with its various irregularities and idiosyncracies, we shall have to accustom ourselves to dealing with factors which do not exist in consciousness at all. Strange as it may seem to the uninitiated, many of our thoughts, ideas, and motives are quite outside our normal consciousness, and of them only the resulting emotions and actions appear on the surface. This may be taken as an absolute and indisputable fact, and one which the reader should try to appreciate at the outset, although it is somewhat difficult to realise, for we always find it hard to apprehend and understand something which we can neither see nor touch.

If one were to tell the ordinary labourer that water is composed of two gases which when combined form a liquid, he would probably be quite incredulous, and possibly in his ignorance might even deny emphatically any such possibility, on the grounds that it was against all common-sense and experience; he failing to realise, of course, how very limited were both his sense and his experience. In spite of his feelings of absolute certainty, and in spite of complete faith in the unshakable logic behind his belief, he would be wrong.

While it is not to be expected that many readers of this book will deny the existence of the unconscious part of the mind, it may well be that many will fail to realise that it is of more than theoretical value. It therefore becomes necessary for us to examine the matter somewhat carefully, and to familiarise ourselves with the ideas of the working of this unconscious mind.

Without going into the further sub-divisions recognised in psychology, we will confine ourselves to dividing the mind into two parts—the conscious and the unconscious. *And of these, at any given moment, the conscious is by far the smaller part.* We are actually conscious at any moment of but very few things, such as the book we are reading, the chair we are sitting on, and dimly of our immediate surroundings. A thousand memories which we might conjure up of our childhood and our past are, for the time being, far from consciousness. Yet these matters exist somewhere in the mind, for we are able, if we choose, to search about in it, and bring them into consciousness, even though we may not have thought of them for many years. This leads us at once to a striking fact, namely, that while many things can be remembered at will, others which we feel we ought to remember, cannot be brought to mind at all. It is an extremely common experience to find that one has forgotten a name completely, and that no effort will bring it into consciousness, yet later on, apparently without effort, the name will "come back to us," as we say. In fact, the very phrase we use—"come back to us"—implies that it has been somewhere away from us, that it has been lodged in some place that is foreign and unknown to us, yet which we are aware is somewhere within us.

It is also common knowledge that a great many events and scenes of considerable importance to us at the time of action are forgotten, and that they can only be recollected if some sort of stimulus or reminder be given. For instance, a person may have forgotten completely where and how he spent a holiday ten years ago. No amount of racking his brain brings anything to light. But having been reminded of a single incident that occurred during that holiday, the whole of the rest may come up from the unconscious in full detail.

There is a third kind of memory more important still, if one may be permitted to call it memory, and that is the memory of facts which no *ordinary* stimulus of this sort will ever bring up into consciousness again. The term "memory" is used here because we have every reason to believe that somewhere in the unconscious all facts have been registered, and in many cases may be partially brought into consciousness again by suitable means, such for instance, as hypnotism or psycho-analysis, (two very different methods, by the way). Yet, though these impressions have been made on the mind, and though there is this unconscious memory still in existence, in the ordinary course of events we should never again be conscious of them.

We may, however, be very conscious of actions and emotions emanating from the unconscious memory. Thus, suppose that as a child one had lived in the country, and on several very happy occasions a bonfire had been lighted at a picnic, and that later on one lived in a town, and that this picnic which happened at the age of three or four years had become completely forgotten, so much so that even photographs of the scenes or conversations on the subject carried on by other people brought no memory to light and seemed to touch no chord; it would still be quite likely that the mere smell of a bon-fire in the distance or any smell resembling this would be enough to cause a considerable feeling of elation and happiness in the person, a feeling that something pleasant was taking place, an idea that if only one could remember, a pleasant picture could be called up. This is because it is associated in the unconscious mind with these previous happy occasions.

Or again, suppose a child at the age of two or three years has been dropped into a pond and nearly drowned. Although the incident may in later years be completely forgotten, the horror of deep water and all its associations may vividly persist. It seems probable, and a considerable amount of work has been done on this subject in psycho-analysis, that every action, thought, or idea that has ever been registered in the mind, even to some extent before birth, is permanently fixed; and that although much of this cannot be brought into consciousness by present methods, yet all the feelings and emotions, however slight, which attended these thoughts, ideas, and actions are perpetually being called forth by slight stimuli of which we are unaware, and these are playing their part in moulding our thoughts, feelings and actions in the present time.

I had an interesting patient a short time ago who, owing to certain experiences in the war, was suffering from complete loss of memory; so complete that he did not know his own wife nor even his parents. Under hypnosis, the whole of his memory was rapidly brought back; and when it appeared to be normal and both he and his parents were quite confident that it was as good as it had ever been, I suggested that we might try an experiment to see if we could improve it still further. I asked him, amongst other things, if he could voluntarily remember the first time he wore knickerbockers. He had not the faintest recollection of the matter. I then hypnotised him, and told him to give me the details. He described the knickerbockers minutely, the number of buttons on them, the fact that he wore them on his third birthday, that his father had given him a penny, and told him that "now he was a little man, he must have money in his pocket," together with a very large number of other details. I enquired of his father and mother and sisters, and they corroborated the details in every particular.

I have tried several similar experiments with him and with one or two other patients under hypnosis with considerable success, and have even tried to take them back to the memory of their own birth. They have frequently produced many memories of events that occurred before the age of one year, but previous to that could only give reproductions of movements and pleasant and unpleasant emotions. Whether these latter are memories or not one has unfortunately no means of proving. But the fact that under hypnosis both educated and uneducated people alike exhibit extremely similar ideas as to types of movements, expressions, and feelings at the various stages of their very early life, inclines one to think that these reproductions may be memories. One has, however, to beware of the fact that observation and knowledge acquired in later periods of their lives might be the real factor underlying their apparent reproductions. Further evidence of a different nature will be given on this point, however, at a later stage in the book.

§2

So far, we have shown that there is an unconscious part of the mind which acts as a store-house for memories, ideas, and emotions of the past. We have not, however, shown that it is anything more than a store-house. But if we look into it from other points of view, we shall see that it is a great deal more than a mere store-house, for it thinks, reasons, comes to conclusions, and in fact assists in controlling our acts at every turn; indeed this unconscious part of our mind wields driving forces of the utmost potency in moulding our lives.

Let us examine first the *reasoning* faculty of the unconscious mind.

Maeder gives a good example of this. A house-surgeon at a hospital wished particularly to keep a certain appointment, but he was not allowed to leave the hospital until his chief, who was out, should return later in the evening. As his appointment was of considerable importance, he decided to brave the anger of his chief. He therefore kept his appointment, but when he returned later, he found to his astonishment that he had left a light in his room, a thing he had never done before, although he had occupied that room for two years. He thought the matter over, and soon realised why he had done this. The chief, on going to his own house, would pass the window and would see the light burning within, and imagine that his house-surgeon was at home. The unconscious mind had rapidly reasoned this out and had determined that the conscious mind should forget to turn off the light.

Another illustration of the persistent way in which the unconscious mind will reason and act can be given from my own experience. I had to attend a lecture given by a man, with whose views I totally disagreed. I had no wish to attend the lecture, but felt compelled to do so in an official capacity. Consciously, I determined to go; unconsciously when I made the note of the lecture, I wrote down the time of it in my engagement-book a week late. On discovering this, I consciously endeavoured to rectify the matter, but my unconscious mind wrote Tuesday instead of Thursday in my engagement-book, so it went down wrong once again. Later, having been forced to see my mistake by a friend mentioning the matter, I omitted for a short time to rectify it in my engagement-book, feeling sure that I should remember to do so a little later. But alas! for the determination of my conscious mind. I forthwith made an appointment for a patient at the real time appointed for the lecture, and so could not in the end attend it. Now, these lectures were held regularly on a particular day of the week, and I had generally looked forward to them, and attended them without any difficulty. It was only in this one case that I did not wish to go. My conscious mind decided to attend; but my unconscious mind played trick after trick in order that my real desires should be satisfied. Such examples could be multiplied indefinitely. It is possible that many would say that they do not actually prove unconscious reasoning nor power of thought. Let me, therefore, give one or two simple examples of a different nature.

A friend of mine once told me that he had spent several days in trying to work out a chess problem without success. One morning, he woke up with a picture in his mind of the exact moves that he must make. The problem had been solved in his sleep unconsciously, and with no recollection on waking of any conscious effort at reaching the solution.

In my own experience, as a school-boy, I failed to solve a problem in Euclid during an examination. On the morning afterwards, the solution flashed through my brain suddenly, as I lay in bed. Whether I had solved it in my sleep, or whether it was solved in bed as I lay awake, I am not prepared to say. Of this much, however, I am certain. I made no conscious effort; my mind merely wandered lazily in the direction of the previous day's failure, and almost instantaneously the right solution appeared without effort.

Let us now take another example of work which the unconscious mind is called upon to perform; an example which we are accustomed to view without question or thought, which is comparatively commonplace, and which we dismiss summarily by referring to it as "habit." The accomplished pianist reads the music in front of him consciously, but he is not conscious of the extremely rapid translation which takes place from the brain to the fingers, so as to produce complicated movements on the key-board. And if we examine it carefully, we shall find that something very wonderful has actually taken place outside his consciousness. When he was first learning to play, he looked at the note on his music, and said to himself "That is C." He looked at the key on the piano, and repeated "That is C." He was taught that a particular finger must be placed on that particular note when playing in a certain key. He was taught that it had to be hit in a particular way and held down for a particular time, according to the size and shape of the note he was reading on the sheet of music in front of him. He was further taught that in order to modify any sound in a particular manner, he could use his feet on one or other of the pedals, and must be extremely careful to put his feet down and lift his feet up again at exactly the right moment. He was taught that when certain symbols, known as sharps and flats, preceded the notes at the beginning of his piece of music, the whole scheme of fingering would be different. And, at first, he had laboriously to go through the process of watching first the music and then the key-board, and of *thinking* at each point what he should do with his fingers and with his feet, and how he should do it, and for what period he should keep on doing it. Now, the whole process is gone through with half-a-million notes which he has never seen before, many of them played simultaneously, and with an exactitude which he never attained when he was consciously thinking. Whatever may be the nature of the unconscious action which is taking place, all he has in consciousness is the music in front of him, and the final sound that he is producing, together with the emotions which these called forth in him as a result of the whole.

Can there be any doubt left that a complicated unconscious process of the same kind is taking place?

Or again, let us examine our own personal likes and dislikes. Frequently one can assign no reason whatsoever for these. They may exist, in fact, against what we call our better judgment. We may love a person in spite of certain faults, or dislike him in spite of his virtues. If the matter be examined further, however, we not infrequently find the reasons for our emotions towards him. Either his manner, dress, or tone of voice, or some other trivial feature may resemble someone we have liked before, or on the contrary, some mannerism may call to mind a similar mannerism which we associate either in ourselves or in some other person, with unpleasant characteristics. Our unconscious mind has rapidly sized up all these points, appraised them, and presented our conscious mind with the resulting emotions alone.

So-called intuition is, to a large extent, merely rapid unconscious reasoning, in which minute details are taken into consideration by the unconscious, and only the final opinion presented to consciousness. One should beware of trusting intuition too much, however, in spite of popular prejudice to the contrary, for unconscious reasoning is just as liable to be wrong in its conclusions as is conscious reasoning; and it is just as liable to reach the conclusion which best serves its immediate purpose, and to suppress truth where it is unpleasant.[1]

Some psychologists think that the unconscious mind is *infallible* in purely *deductive* reasoning from the *premises* from which it starts. But it provides its own premises from a secret store and also accepts any suggested premises which are not repugnant. The premises may therefore be wrong but the deductive reasoning is accurate. In this case the conclusions will only be wrong because the premises are wrong.

---

[1] Unconscious reasoning or intuition is found chiefly in those who have not been trained in subjects which induce and train logical conscious reasoning. It is not a prerogative of sex, but on the whole is found more amongst women, merely because of their method of training from childhood upwards. In children and savages intuition is found equally present in both sexes. The loss of intuition merely means that the training of the conscious mind has caused us to mistrust conclusions for which we cannot consciously see the reasons.

Chapter 2. Repression

§1

One other faculty of the unconscious mind requires special mention, and that is its power of obliterating memories from the conscious mind, or as it is better termed, of *repressing*, since this word not only implies pushing out of consciousness, but also preventing from coming into consciousness. It is found that all persons have formed a regular habit of forgetting or partially forgetting, (and so disguising), things which are unpleasant to them. This especially refers to those things which are unpleasant to their self-respect, their moral beliefs and ideas, and their general pride in themselves. The primitive immoralities and thoughts and actions of early childhood which would now offend their æsthetic and moral susceptibilities, are, more or less, completely put out of sight, together with a host of unpleasant ideas and thoughts which have cropped up from childhood onwards. Indeed, there is a general tendency for anything of an unpleasant nature to be pushed out of sight.

Darwin, in his autobiography, states, "I had, during many years, followed a golden rule, namely that whenever a published fact, a new observation or thought came across me, which was opposed to my general results, to make a memorandum of it without fail, and at once, for I had found by experience that such facts and thoughts were far more apt to escape from the memory than favourable ones."

We had a further example in the case of the house-surgeon who "forgot" to put out his light, and examples are extremely common in everyday life. We forget to post letters entrusted to us against our will, but we do not forget to post our own love-letters. We mislay bills very readily, but rarely do we mislay a cheque.

Amongst my patients suffering from shell-shock, I have had very many hundreds who have completely forgotten some of the most unpleasant and terrifying experiences which occurred to them out at the front. Others unconsciously had found the easiest method of dealing with the unpleasant past to be that of blotting the whole of it out, dissociating it completely from their conscious mind, and then stating that they remembered nothing of their lives until they woke up in hospital. It is not only memories, however, which are repressed and remain dormant in the unconscious mind. Most of our primitive instincts handed on from our savage forefathers before even the evolution of man in his present form, lie similarly buried in this unconscious part of the mind, and we are wont to deny emphatically that we possess these unpleasant instincts. Nevertheless, just as *in utero* we repeat more or less in detail the history of our physical evolution, so do we at that period and in childhood repeat to a great extent the history of our psychic evolution; and just as during this early period we possess the physical attributes of many of our ancestors, such as the gills of the fish or the tail of the lower vertebrates, so psychically do we at a somewhat later period, possess the instincts and desires of our progenitors, and utilise them as the hidden foundation stones in building our adult mental constitution. These various primitive instincts include all kinds of desires which would consciously be regarded as sexual perversions and moral crimes of different kinds, and they are present in all of us without exception. Our upbringing and conscious outlook upon them, however, causes them to be so abhorrent to us, that we successfully keep the majority of such ideas and feelings *from ever coming out of the unconscious in their primitive form*. In other words, we repress them. Occasionally, however, there is a tendency for these ancestral instincts to become conscious, and in our further efforts to prevent this we may develop instead hysterias, obsessions and unreasonable fears, together with many other nervous and abnormal signs and symptoms, into the nature of which it is not my intention to inquire further in this present volume. Those who are interested in pursuing this line of investigation will find an elementary account of it in a previous work of mine, "The Elements of Practical Psycho-Analysis." All that I wish to emphasise here is that we do push out from the conscious mind unpleasant thoughts and memories, that we do repress and keep in the unconscious mind unpleasant desires and instincts, and that we do, as a result of this, have many unconscious or semi-conscious conflicts within ourselves, which may lead to unpleasant feelings of depression, irritability, fear, or in more pronounced cases hysterias, obsessions, and even permanent mental derangement.

§2

A further and somewhat important result of our possessing so much which is unconscious and of having so many feelings and ideas in consciousness of which we do not know the origin, or of whose origins we have but the vaguest and haziest notion is known as *rationalization*. This word signifies that we find reasons for doing or believing things which are of a pleasant nature and agreeable to us, and *vice versa*.

Following on this rationalisation comes also a certain conservatism, which tends to retard progress of any sort, which dislikes looking at new ideas, and this for a very obvious reason. Looking at new ideas, examining ourselves or our work very closely, has a tendency to bring to light, from time to time, the very primitive instincts and feelings which we have been at so much pains to repress. And rather than submit to the indignity of discovering how really imperfect we are, and having our pride in our divinely constituted natures shaken, we have acquired a habit of denying and fighting strenuously against discovering truths connected with either our moral or physical evolution which would be unpleasant to us. In the light of our upbringing, such new truths are often unpleasant, therefore we rationalise that they must be untrue. For having been educated to venerate logic and reason, we can only be satisfied with any given conclusion we come to when we feel that it is justifiable in the light of logic and reason. But the logic of rationalisation is false logic.

For many years, scientific and popular thought denied strenuously the possibility of the now universally accepted theory of human evolution; and on scientific grounds it was urged, with much plausible reasoning, that it was not possible to develop a high type like man from any low form of animal. On religious grounds it was argued equally passionately that if evolution were true, the Bible was wrong, God disappeared, and therefore the theory of evolution was untrue. The real reasons lying behind those reasons advanced by both the scientist and the general public, however, were not the reasons so carefully thought out by them, but consisted largely in the fact that they did not wish to find that the body, which they had hitherto thought a special and divine creation partaking of the miraculous, to be merely a stage in the evolution of life on this planet, and possibly not a final stage at that. For in that case, no longer would man be able to flatter himself that he was almost divine, he would have to relegate himself to the possibility of being in a stage of semi-barbarism; he would no longer be a final perfect product, but merely a half-finished article. It was this blow to his pride that he could not stand. And it is the same to-day. Whenever there is a likelihood that examination, particularly through research work, has thrown light on his psychic evolution, on the imperfections of his moral laws, or on the crudity of some conventional custom, the process which takes place in him is much the same.

Firstly, dislike of the idea. Secondly, on further examination of it, hatred of the idea. Thirdly, rationalisation directed against the idea. Fourthly, contentment, in that he has proved by logic and reason that the idea is wrong. Hence, it is that the truth takes long to emerge, and that obsessions and hysterias, and even trivial abnormalities are difficult to cure, for the cure involves seeing our own imperfections naked and undisguised.

In all these cases, we are trying to keep out of consciousness those things which will distress us or cause us to have conflicts, or to have to readjust our views of ourselves, or in fact cause us unpleasantness in any form. It will be noticed that I have mentioned pride in the belief that we have reached a condition of final development, and in our superiority over the rest of nature, as being one of the important factors in preventing our advance. It is to the development of this pride, and its ramifications that I am devoting the major portion of this book.

Chapter 3. The Forces Shaping Character

It will be seen from the foregoing that evolution of the individual character may be the result of a very large number of forces at work, of which many are quite unconscious; and that any considerable disturbance or variation of the unconscious factors will considerably modify the character of the individual, in spite of conscious desires in some other direction. The character of an individual is the sum of his thoughts, ideas, capacities, desires, feelings and actions, and the general forces moulding it may be briefly summarised as follows:

1. The primitive instincts inherited from his ancestors, and held back in the unconscious mind.

2. Environment and education.

3. That pride in his own greatness, to which we referred in the last chapter, which modifies all the other forces at work, according to the direction of its development. This force will henceforth be called by the name of Narcissism, for a reason shortly to be explained.

§2

Of the inherited instincts we have already said as much as is necessary here. It suffices for us to recognise that they are for the most part of a primitive erotic type, and that they are so repressed and modified as to be unrecognisable in the normal adult. When they have been ineffectually converted by environment and education, we have present the basis of many neurotic and functional conditions, and this again is a matter which is outside the scope of the present work.

§3

Environment and education are extremely comprehensive terms as used in psychology. Environment does not merely refer to the home with its visible surroundings, nor does education merely refer to the scholastic side of it. Environment and education include the treatment of the child by the nurse during the first week of life; for instance, whether she leaves it alone when it cries, or whether she soothes it and rocks it to sleep again. A trivial fact, the reader will think, especially in the first week of the child's life, yet experience shows us that this environment and education of the first week is an extremely important factor in its after-life. The thousand little actions, the trivial chance words of anger or contempt, not merely of the parent but of strangers or of other children, all make their impressions on the infantile unconscious mind. They all belong, in the strictest sense, to what we term its environment and education. Any stimulus, in fact, however small, which is capable of reaching the brain forms part of this environment and education which is reacting on the child. Psychologists are now generally of the opinion that the essential elements of the individual character have all been definitely formed by the age of five, and that, important as training in successive years may be, the environment and education during those first five years are more important still.

It is the object of education and environment to modify and utilise the force of the primitive instincts with which the child comes into the world in the best possible way.

Three things may happen to any particular instinct. Firstly, it may remain unchanged and unrepressed, in which case the individual will be said, on reaching adult life, to be perverted in some way. Let us take as an example that instinct which exists in some animals, and which urges them at the mating season to exhibit their genital organs to their fellows of the opposite sex, with the perfectly natural and proper end in view of propagating the species. We occasionally find adult human beings in whom this instinct has remained unchanged and uncontrolled, and they generally find their way, sooner or later, into prison. The psychological term for the offence they commit is "exhibitionism." In the small child, however, we have often seen this instinct at work, without regarding it as objectionable in any way. We have laughed at the little child who delights in running about naked, or asks us to come and see it being bathed, or on occasion calls even more obvious attention to its state of nakedness. It is quite unconscious of the primitive instinct which it is displaying, and since it is a child and cannot in any way fulfil the sexual objects of the instinct, we pass the matter over, without further thought.

Secondly, our primitive instincts may be *displaced*, and the displacement must be such as to conceal them from our conscious thoughts, in order that they may be tolerated by the conscious mind. For instance, the normal adult will not be guilty of exhibiting his nakedness in the way above referred to, nor will he display desires of sexual exhibitionism in a conscious manner. But he, or more frequently she, will *displace* these ideas, and will only call attention to the sex of her body indirectly by exhibiting the neck or arms, or more indirectly still through the medium of clothes, designed to suggest, (for the most part unconsciously) erotic ideas.

Thirdly, a much higher state may be reached by some people in which the primitive instinct has now lost entirely its erotic meaning, instead of being merely disguised and displaced as in the last case. The force and energy of it has all gone from the personal physical plane to serve a useful social purpose of a non-sexual nature. This is known as *sublimation*, and instead of the desire of our exhibitionist to show himself or herself physically, the person may attain the desire by showing a fine character, by designing a fine building, achieving some high position, or anything in fact of an ideal or non-erotic nature.

Exactly the same process takes place in the opposite of exhibitionism, which in its primitive form we term observationism. "Peeping Tom" is a celebrated example of this. We have a *displacement* of observationism in the fairly average young man, who likes to observe all that he can of the charms of every woman he comes into contact with, who takes an eager interest in her shoulders, breasts, underclothing, and any part she may exhibit. And we have the third or *sublimated* stage in the scientist, who has turned most of his primitive sexual instinct of "looking" in the sexual sense into looking down the microscope, or searching for the secrets of Nature, and delving amidst her hidden laws, instead of using the same primitive desire to look in an unsublimated and rather more infantile manner.

It is exactly the same with a large number of other primitive instincts, which even did I mention them here would not be grasped or understood at all by many without very much further explanation. Suffice it to say, that many of our higher activities and desires are sublimations of lower and more primitive instincts, which we are learning to develop and control; *and that education and environment have, as their object, the training of the child by turning the forces at work in his primitive instincts through the stage of displacement into the final one of sublimation.*

It should be clearly grasped that the energy lying behind our primitive instincts, whether it be repressed, displaced or sublimated, is a very real force, comparable with the physical energy which we are accustomed to deal with in everyday life. *And this energy must find some outlet for its discharge.* Thus,[2] "We know as regards physical energy that there are not several kinds of energy, but merely several manifestations of it, and that it may be changed from one form of manifestation to another, but that still the sum total of the original energy remains without addition or loss."

Thus there is a given amount of energy stored in a ton of coal. This energy can manifest itself as *heat* in the furnace and boiler. By means of an engine we can change the manifestation into that of *motion*, then with a dynamo to *electricity*; the electricity we can again change into *light*, or back again into *heat* or *motion*. There is *one* energy, but by suitable means we can turn it to different uses, and give different manifestations of it. Owing, however, to the imperfection of the boiler, machinery, etc., we never transform the *whole* of our energy into another form. In transforming heat into electricity, there is always some heat wasted; it is not destroyed, but it remains as heat for a time, and is absorbed by surrounding objects. A complete transference of energy does not take place, and the less efficient the machinery the less is the transference.

Now evidence tends to show a considerable similarity between psychic and physical energy. In all probability there is only one ultimate psychic energy which, like physical energy, can be directed into different channels. Thus, the energy of erotic desire can be directed to a large extent into the energy of desire for music, religion, science, or sport; or the energy of the desire for sport may be changed into the energy of the desire for mental exercise, such as chess, mathematics, or science. For example, an individual feels "restless," he then desires to play tennis; the afternoon is wet: he plays chess instead. His psychic energy has been diverted from one channel into another with its accompanying excitement and satisfaction of desire: with its final feeling of fatigue and repletion.

Psychic energy, like physical energy, can never be entirely diverted from one channel to another. There is always some, often a large quantity, which is not altered in character. The amount of this depends largely on the person concerned, just as the amount of physical energy, changed from one form to another depends on the efficiency of the engine or machinery.

This possibility of transference of energy of desire from one form to another is of the utmost importance to the psycho-analyst. By the technique of psycho-analysis the energy of repressed desires is first freed from deleterious objectives, and then transferred to legitimate ones. The energy behind the conflicts which lead to alcoholism or drug-taking may, under suitable conditions, be transferred to energy of higher types of desire with more suitable outlets. These processes are known as *transference* and *sublimation* respectively.

---

[2] "Elements of Practical Psycho-Analysis," by Paul Bousfield.

It may be taken that every mind has a given amount of psychic energy which *must* find somewhere its suitable outlet in satisfying desire, whether for accomplishment or for enjoyment.

We may here again take the opportunity of stating that the efficiency or lack of efficiency demonstrated in different individuals in their attempts to transfer the energy of desire from a lower to a higher channel depends not only on heredity and constitutional circumstances but to an extraordinary degree on the individual's environment and the actions of the parents in the first three or four years of his life. The reason why seemingly excellent parents produce sometimes execrable progeny becomes clearer under psycho-analysis. The over-strict parent produces one type of inefficient children, the parent who spoils produces other inefficient types. The nurse, the nursery, the casual visitor, the trivial conversations, the unconsidered sights and experiences, all have a terrific influence in the first few years of the child's life. Parents do not realise that conventional or arbitrary methods of education, whether in one direction or another, are not going to effect the results they expected. The primitive unconscious mind of the child understands and absorbs in a manner that civilised man does not recognise. The bad father may by accident or *neglect* produce an excellent child—the good father with all his designs may produce a bad one. This is not an attempt to show that as the child grows up *all* its actions are dependent on the early environment; merely that we can never compare the good or bad in individuals; that an apparent failure, owing to his inefficiency of powers of sublimation, may yet be devoting more energy to ascent than the successful saint whose early environment made for efficient transference of energy of desire. Some of the commonest of errors made by well-meaning parents will come to light at a later period. "*They teach their children to repress erotic and other desires but they omit at the same time to assist the development of that sublimation of them which is absolutely essential.*"

§4

We now come to the third great factor in character formation, and as this particular factor is going to occupy the major portion of this book, I will not do more here than indicate briefly the symbolic meaning of the term Narcissism; the reason why this term is used in connection with our primitive feelings of pride will then gradually unfold itself.

Narcissus was the son of the river god, Cephissus. In his mother's eyes he was extremely beautiful, and later in the eyes of all others, including himself. It was his wont to walk abroad in solitary places lost in admiration of the graceful form which he thought no eyes worthy to behold, save his own. On one occasion, he wanted to drink from a cool spring and catching sight of his face in the water for the first time in his life, at once fell in love with it, not knowing it to be his own likeness. On his knees at the edge of the pool, he stretched himself, and looked down upon a face and form so entrancingly beautiful, that he was ready to leap into the water beside it.

"Who art thou, who hast been made so fair?" cried Narcissus. And the lips of the image moved, yet there came no answer. He stretched out his hand towards it, and the beautiful form beckoned to him. But when his hand touched and broke the surface, it vanished like a dream, only to return in all its enchantment when he was content to gaze motionless, even then, again, growing dim beneath the tears of vexation he shed into the water. Repeatedly, he tried to gather the lovely image in his arms, but it always eluded him, but when he entreated and implored, it imitated his gestures with unfeeling silence.

Maddened by the strong allurement of his own likeness, he could not tear himself away from the mirror which ever mocked his fancy. Hour after hour, day after day, he leant over the pool's brink, crying in vain for that imaginary object of adoration. But at last from despair his heart ceased to throb, and he lay still among the water-lilies that made his shroud.

*   *   *   *   *   *   *

Before proceeding further and examining the development of Narcissism, and those factors which come to preserve it, and make it forceful in our unconscious mind, we must first briefly consider the subject of determinism.

Chapter 4. Determinism And Will Power

Determinism is the doctrine that all things, including the will, are determined by causes. It is the antithesis of the doctrine of free will. In its complete form, it holds that the individual has no direct and voluntary control over his thoughts and actions but that every thought and action is inevitably the result of a large number of previous thoughts and actions which have gone before.

There is a very large amount of evidence, and indeed, whether we admit it or not, the evidence is quite irrefutable, that in regard to the majority of our actions the doctrine of determinism holds good. But the evidence is by no means sufficient to enable us to conclude that we have no free will.

[3]Freud in his book on the "Psychopathology of Everyday Life" and in other works gives many convincing examples that much in our character, that many of our actions, evil and good, are quite beyond our control at any given moment. But there is one thing that appears to have been overlooked, and that is, *that in all the examples given one could not conceivably utilise free will in any case.* If I ask you to think of a number what opportunity do you get of using your will power? If you put the wrong latch-key into the door by accident, have you made any effort to use will power? When a patient is suffering from hysteria due to repressions of various kinds, in that particular matter *the will power has already been lost.* When a chronic alcoholic is unable to cease from drinking his will power in reference to this has disappeared, therefore determinism holds the field completely. The will has no opportunity of working then. In all the examples which Freud gives one discovers on careful investigation that for some reason or another there is no opportunity for the use of free will. Such evidence as we have certainly does not prove the nonexistence of free will, but merely shows that in a very large number of our thoughts and actions we do not use any will at all, and that in other cases we are unable to use our will effectively.[4] When determinism does rule we may liken it physically to this: a patient sits down and crosses one leg over the other and leaves the one leg hanging free. On tapping it smartly beneath the patella the foot will kick; the knee jerk has been elicited. If this be done fifty times the result will be the same fifty times. There is movement of the leg, but this movement is predetermined. On the other hand this does not prove that no other movement of the leg is possible. Under the conditions just given the man's will, or the freedom of the leg, is merely *eliminated during that period.* Or again, we may liken it to a locomotive standing at the top of a hill; if the brake be taken off, the locomotive will run down the hill, and will do it every time;

---

[3] "The Elements of Practical Psycho-Analysis," by Paul Bousfield.
[4] The doctrines of determinism and free-will respectively can be brought entirely into line with one another if we include freewill itself as one of the determinants. Thus, if in the formula
$S = a + b + c + d + etc.$
where S is the resultant action, and a, b, c, d, etc., are the several determinants, it happens that d = 0. The presence of d does not invalidate the formula. *But if* d *does not happen to be zero, the absence of* d *would invalidate the formula.* If d represents the "will" component there may be plenty, even a majority of cases in which d = 0, but there may be cases in which the omission of d will render the result erroneous.

but this will not prove that did somebody happen to put the brake on half-way down the hill the engine would still go on running. However, all actions which we may ascribe to our will are no doubt strictly limited by other determined conditions. The man on the engine may run it backwards or forwards, but only within *the very much prescribed limits which the rails allow*. We may safely accept this much determinism, that although the will exists, its capabilities are strictly circumscribed by determinism.

It is rather in his general direction than in any specific act that a man has most control. We certainly have not the amount of free will which we like to believe we have. For example, the reader of this chapter may have returned home to-night and have said, "I will not have a meal to-night, it is too hot." What are the factors (or determinants, as they are called) in this case? Perhaps external heat, producing langour by various physiological processes, combined with lack of appetite, in its turn produced by several causes, and added to this, depression, produced by a bad business deal, and in its turn the result of many other determinants outside the reader's control. There is no desire to eat, and these various determinants, added together, prove stronger than the habit of eating the evening meal. Having, however, read this chapter as far as this point, the reader desiring to disprove my unpleasant suggestion, immediately says, "Ah! I will prove that I have free will. I will eat my meal in spite of not wanting it."

Alas! this does not *prove* free will, new determinants have merely been added on the other side, and desire to prove strength of mind has now out-weighed accumulated efforts which prevented you from eating.

Since it has been shown that a man's control is constantly being limited by other determinants, it follows that the criminal whose environment and determinants, conscious and unconscious, have been manufactured for him from evil sources, yet who, on the whole, is progressing upwards in spite of these, may be forming a far better character than the arch-bishop whose environment from the beginning has been such as never to give him criminal characteristics, yet whose growth has been, on the whole, towards a more selfish position, even though this be not noticeable to the eyes of others.

Now many of the determinants forming our characters lie in the unconscious. They are unknown to us and only the results of their activities are visible. Herein lies the difficulty of controlling ourselves. How can we efficiently control that of which we do not know the existence? Herein, also, lies the value of psycho-analysis, for it brings many of these determinants to light, and we are thus able to control them consciously. Only a part of all this can be accomplished by such self-analysis as may be indicated in this book. Yet even so, a much greater degree of self-control may be obtained.

§2

Let us now consider briefly why persons who have not previously been irritable, should suddenly become irritable; who have not previously been hysterical, should suddenly become hysterical; who have not previously been in the habit of weeping, should at some time after reaching adult life, revert to that infantile habit.

The explanation of mental troubles of various kinds involves two factors. In the first place, any individual is capable of bearing a certain amount of conflict and a certain amount of repression. It is only when the accumulated force is more than he can control, *that is when new determinants are added*, that the symptoms begin to appear. He is like a steam engine in which as long as the steam is being used up in doing work, or as long as the safety valve is working efficiently when work is not being done, the boiler stands a pressure of 100lbs. very comfortably. If the safety valve gets jammed, and the energy cannot be transferred from the steam to the work, the pressure in the boiler rises higher and higher until it bursts from the joints and rivet-holes.

The second factor which determines the mode of expression of this out-burst of repressed energy is known as the *law of regression*. This means that if the adult outlet of energy becomes dammed up or is insufficient, *the energy will flow through an earlier channel which has once been used*. The individual will, in fact, revert to some method which he was wont to use in earlier years, or in infancy. It is true that this may be disguised and not recognised as an infantile mode of expression until it is looked into more closely. This question of regression, however, need not be more than touched upon here. It will be much more fully dealt with when we come to actual examples at a later stage.

Chapter 5. Narcissism

The term Narcissism has already been mentioned and some slight indication of its importance in character development has been given. We have also examined the derivation of the term, and found that it implies self-interest, self-importance, self-worship; all of which characteristics are in modified degrees possessed by everybody. There are, however, many other manifestations of Narcissism, many tricks by which it gets past our conscious intentions, many ways in which it associates itself with other instincts, and unknown to us works our undoing. We shall therefore, in this chapter, examine the development of Narcissism from its very earliest stages, and trace out in some detail whither it may lead.

Most people were they asked at what moment the child's mind first began to register feelings, thoughts, and emotions, would probably at once and without hesitation say, "At the moment of birth." It seems the obvious thing to say, but like many other obvious things such a statement appears to have but little evidence in support of it and much against it.

The act of birth has performed no sudden or miraculous change upon the growth and tissues of the body. It is true that oxygen is now absorbed through the lungs instead of as originally through the mother's blood, but the essential tissues, the brain, the muscles and the bones have undergone no sudden change. Before birth, they were living tissues, and we know that the muscles were at work, for we had felt the baby's movements *in utero*; we know that the heart was at work, driving the blood through the child's arteries. We had learnt this also by means of the stethoscope many weeks before the child was born. Why then should we assume that the brain had registered nothing at birth? We do indeed know that it must have been at work in part, for it was learning to regulate the action of the child's heart and the child's secretions, the blood pressure, and the motions of its limbs. We are therefore justified in assuming that it must be capable of registering impressions, even though it were incapable of reason or thought.

It is true that at birth it commences to undergo many vivid new experiences, but that is no reason for assuming that it has not undergone any experiences *in utero*, and that these experiences have not made some impressions on the brain. Let us see for a moment what impressions it is likely to have received and registered. First of all, it would most certainly hear sounds, the sounds of the blood rushing through the mother's arteries and the sounds from the outer world, muffled and indistinct when they had penetrated the mother's body. All these sounds would be of a soft crooning nature, and those caused by the blood in the mother's arteries would be of a rhythmic, humming, rising and falling nature, a kind of rhythmic lullaby very similar in many respects to the lullaby the mother will hum to the child when she wishes to put it to sleep at a later period. We should expect these sounds to be registered on the child's brain so that if it ever heard their like again, some chord of *feeling-memory* would be struck, and some emotional association brought to mind. In the second place, external movements would be registered on the child's mind as the mother walked about. There would be a swaying or swinging movement. Again we should expect that when, in after life, the child experienced a swaying or swinging movement, a chord of memory would be touched again, and these earlier associations would be revived; not as a conscious memory or fact, of course, but as a feeling.

Again, conscious movements of its own limbs might be impressed upon it. It would find, when it tried to move, that its movements were limited, and that it attained more perfect peace by refraining from attempting to struggle and change its position. It would be impressed by the pleasantness of inertia as opposed to the unpleasantness of making an effort. And finally, its general position with the knees drawn up and the chin bent down would be firmly registered, so that when in after-life it again assumed this position, once more the chord of memory would be struck, and the old feeling of repose would be likely to return.

Now, we cannot assume that the child has any active mental state before its birth, but we know that its condition (taken in conjunction with its extremely limited experience) is one as near omnipotence (from its standpoint) as may be. It breathes, or rather absorbs oxygen without any effort of breathing. It is fed, it is kept warm and comfortable without any effort whatsoever. It lives in a world entirely its own, where everything works together for its comfort and well-being. It has to make no struggle for existence. It has to deal with nothing *real*, save perhaps that its voluntary movements are limited, and this perhaps is bad for its education, since at that period of its life it learns that it can be most comfortable by making least effort! And here we see the beginning of that which we all possess in after-life, *inertia*, the difficulty of making a beginning at anything, the objection which we have to making efforts.

Now let us see what happens to this omnipotent little creature at birth. It goes through the probably painful process of having its position roughly changed and being thrust into an atmosphere which is cold and unusual to it. Moreover it has to make its first struggle for breath, its first effort to sustain existence. And in its struggle for breath it utters cries, which by experience it very soon finds to be magic sounds which enable it to fulfil its wishes. But of this, more later.

After its first rude awakening, let us once more see what happens. It is wrapped up in something warm; that is, it is returned to a semblance of the womb, by having something round it which keeps out the cold. It is gently rocked to and fro by the nurse or other attendant, and again the semblance of the previous rocking in the womb is returned to it. Crooning sounds are murmured over it, and the semblance is still more complete. It frequently draws its knees up somewhat if it is placed in such a position that it can do so with ease, and falls asleep. It has attained as nearly as possible once more the semblance of its pre-birth condition, where it has no cares, and is warm and comfortable again. And though it has become acquainted with effort, it is quite obvious that its feeling of omnipotence, if we may so term it for the moment, is hardly yet disturbed, and the world it has come into differs but slightly from the world which it has left; it is still a world in which the infant is the centre and ruler, in which its every want is attended to without an effort on its part, save that it may sometimes have to call attention to its wants by means of that magical cry which it soon learns how and when to use, and which acts in a truly magical manner in accomplishing the fulfilment of all its desires.

During the first few weeks of the infant's life this delusion on the part of the child is largely kept up. Few people think there is any harm in attending to all a baby's wants in the first month of its life. They do not think it could possibly be wrong to spoil it at that age, because its intellect has not developed. They forget entirely that its mental condition and attitude towards life, apart from actual thought, may inevitably be affected at this period. Hence, whenever the baby cries, it is not uncommonly rocked to sleep, or fed, or if it holds out its hand and shows its desire to possess anything, it is immediately allowed to possess it, and to play with it. It has to make but the faintest attempts to adjust itself to its environment, it has to face but the slightest reality; all its desires are immediately fulfilled, and kept in a condition of almost continual fulfilment. And it may remain for a considerable period as near being an omnipotent creature as it is possible for any living thing to be. Its omnipotence, however, is really a fallacy, or as I prefer to term it at a slightly later stage, a phantasy, for the world in which it lived before birth, which seemed to it as a world, was not really a world at all, but a very small and a very temporary abode, and the world in which it is living for the first few months after birth is again not really a world but a combination of extremely limited and carefully selected portions of the world, in which every attempt is made to disguise from it the realities of the actual world.

Again let us emphasise the fact that the chief effort that the infant has to make is the effort of crying. And it may learn very quickly that this is so all-powerful as to practically efface the unpleasant task of having to adjust itself to the realities of life. This process is carried on with slight modifications for many months. The infant has but to wave a magic wand, as it were, has but to emit a little magic noise from its mouth, and all the world it knows is set in motion to give it satisfaction and some semblance of its pre-birth omnipotence.

This cry which brings it gratification, if it has been really effective over a too-prolonged period, will tend to fix permanently in the child's mind the fact that either weeping or making a magic noise with the mouth will always attain for it gratification. And although at a later stage the conscious mind will be obliged to accept a considerable amount of reality and to reject the idea of omnipotence, yet the unconscious mind will persist in the struggle and will make futile efforts to forget reality, to change reality into phantasy, and to regain its omnipotent state.

When a man uses expletives because some task of his has failed to result in success, he is really repeating the infant's cry. He is really uttering a magic sound which his unconscious mind hopes may somehow remedy the failure. He has not definitely accepted the reality of failure as a commonplace hard fact of life at the moment at which he utters his expletive.

When a person weeps at some unpleasant happening or in anger at something which has touched his pride, exactly the same is taking place. He, or she, has failed to make a complete adaptation of himself to the facts and realities of life. *He has obeyed the law of regression*, to which I referred in a previous chapter, and has returned to the infantile method of expression, namely weeping, with the unconscious hope that a magic compensation will result; that instead of his having to adapt himself to the facts of life, the facts of life will somehow adapt themselves to his phantasy.

Hence, the first piece of advice that one must give to parents is that they should, from the earliest possible moment, train the infant to understand that the magic cries will not at once produce their expected result; and the first week in the infant's life is all-important in this matter. The choosing of the nurse who has charge during that period should be done with great care, and what is required of her should be insisted on. Too great emphasis cannot be laid upon these points.

The child should be fed at regular and proper intervals, and should be kept warm. But if it cries, as it will do naturally, it should be left to itself to cry. It should not be picked up, rocked to sleep, given another meal nor petted. If it is left to cry, it will learn very rapidly and at the right period of its life that the sounds which it emits are not magical, and it will begin to adapt itself to the fact that it lives in a real world which has not been built solely and only for its own delight.

It is curious to note how regression, this instinct to return to the earlier mode of expression, to return apparently even to the pre-birth state, persists in the unconscious mind.

During the war, I knew a youth who was intensely agitated by the air-raids. He felt perfectly safe, however, if he could crawl under the bed or table, where he would curl himself into practically the same position as that of a normal baby before birth. When questioned, he had not, of course, the slightest conscious knowledge of why he felt safe in such curious circumstances. But it does not seem improbable that the association of ideas produced by his position and by the confined space created a feeling akin to that feeling of safety which has been his in his pre-birth omnipotent position where nothing could harm him. A similar feeling of security was experienced by many normal persons in cellars and other confined spaces and was probably of the same origin; for there is no doubt that this safety was felt even though their reason told them that a bomb was as likely to reach their confined space as any other place in the neighbourhood.

Again, I know of innumerable cases in which soldiers felt very much safer from bombs which fell at night when they were under cover of a canvas tent. Logically, of course, the thing was absurd; emotionally, it was a fact. And all were equally unconscious of any possible reasons for the feeling of security produced. An example of this same tendency at an earlier age is seen in children who cover their heads with the bedclothes when they are frightened.

To return to our Narcissistic infant, we are now impressed with the fact that one thing of the utmost importance in the first years of its life is that it shall gradually come into contact with reality, shall discover that all things do not belong to it, that its omnipotent feelings are based purely upon phantasy and not upon reality; and upon the method of its disillusionment and the age at which this begins largely depend the future powers of adaptation of the child to its surroundings. It has now become obvious that the new-born infant lives in a world of phantasy, in which, the relative importance of itself to things outside itself is not merely distorted but is entirely absent. And if we can suppose a child kept artificially in this condition till it reached adult life, every wish satisfied instantaneously, every force it knows directed entirely towards gratifying its immediate desires, we do not require much imagination to understand how absolutely helpless and lost this omnipotent creature would be if suddenly turned into the world to face life and reality. His one desire would be to return to his omnipotent state, his one effort to keep at bay reality and turn it into the pleasant phantasy of the previous twenty years. For he would surely, before his disillusionment, have really come to believe himself omnipotent, the only real thing in a phantasy world of his own fashioning and dreaming.

An extreme case of this kind is, of course, an impossibility. But there are many and various degrees in which it is approached. Probably the nearest approach to it may be found in cases where some sort of moral or mental conflict has been too much for an extremely Narcissistic mind, which has then completely regressed, refused to recognise the outer world, and developed a certain form of insanity; and from this stage of complete Narcissistic regression all degrees and kinds of manifestations of it may be found, until we reach at the other end of our list a person who expects everyone around to consult his wishes and peculiarities or who is merely somewhat impatient, or inclined to irritability, or merely over-sensitive to either mental or physical pain.

There is no more certain fact than that if an infant be allowed to postpone its acquaintance with reality too long it becomes fixed in a more or less degree in conditions in which phantasy plays too prominent a part, and regression of some kind takes place as it meets with real difficulties.

Chapter 6. Fact And Phantasy

In the last chapter we emphasised the fact that one of the first products of Narcissism was the infantile difficulty of distinguishing between fact and phantasy, of realising the world outside oneself. This tendency to mix up fact with phantasy is by no means only to be found in an abnormal mind. It is present in some degree in all persons; each one feels himself to be the most real thing present, and in feeling this he has a tendency to believe that others round him are in some way less real, though, fortunately, very few carry it far enough to imagine that all the others are merely part of a dream in which the dreamer is the only real figure, as the Red King in "Alice Through the Looking Glass" is supposed to have done, when the remark is made to Alice, "You're only a sort of thing in his dream! If that there king was to wake you would go out bang—just like a candle!"

And yet quite a large number of people find it difficult to realise firstly, that they must die, and secondly that the rest of the world will not die also when they die. They know, of course, that this latter is not the case, yet they cannot look upon it as a commonplace fact. Their Narcissism refuses to contemplate their own mortality. It represses the fact and leaves the idea vague and unreal to them.

In children, the difficulty of distinguishing between phantasy and reality is quite normally much more accentuated than in adults. And since they start in a world of phantasy and their training is to lead them to a world of reality, it is obvious that the halfway stages will be obscured by a strange mixture of the two. All children go through the stage in which phantasy and reality are by no means clearly differentiated, and most young children succeed, day by day, in fulfilling impossible wishes in phantasies in a manner which a properly developed adult can never do.

A little boy desires to possess a pony; if this be impossible his imagination gives life to a rocking-horse, and failing that he may tie a piece of string to a chair, and with great pleasure and much emotion urge on his fiery untamed steed across mountain and desert. He fulfils his wishes immediately by means of a phantasy, which, for the time being, successfully replaces reality. If this child grows up normally, this possibility of phantastic fulfilment should gradually disappear. How many adults, for instance, could take a bath-tub into their dining-room, sit in it, and with the aid of a vivid imagination thoroughly enjoy a pleasant sail at sea? We trust no one, at any rate of our readers, for they would be of that type which has no perspective, and they would most certainly fail in their vocation as practical men and women. Yet remnants of phantasy thinking remain with everyone, and in a moderate degree, so far as we know, such remnants do but little harm if they are present in small measure only, and kept in water-tight compartments.

Adult phantasy thinking very largely consists in what is known as identification, which may be either conscious or unconscious. Of this, we shall have more to say shortly. At the moment let us trace out what should happen to the normal child as it grows older. Education and environment should be gradually convincing the child of the unreality of its phantastic thoughts and of its early world, should be inducing it to think in terms of facts and to adjust himself to these facts, instead of attempting the impossible task of adjusting these facts to suit his own phantastic conceptions of them. The method of thought which he should develop in order thus to fit himself to meet the world adequately has been conveniently termed "directive thinking." Directive thinking is controlled thought based upon facts seen in their true perspective, and with a purpose in view which is both definite and possible. It is the very opposite of phantasy thinking, which is generally indefinite, based upon a lack of perspective, and attempts continually to obtain the fulfilment of wishes impossible of fulfilment.

In directive thinking, the purpose in view must be purposive to the thinker, a change to be produced in the world, either in its happiness, its morals, its commercial prosperity or in other forms of progress or even of deterioration; or the purpose may be to effect changes in the individual's own happiness or prosperity, or it may be directed towards a mental change in the thinker himself with no immediate idea of changes in his external surroundings.

Thus a man may wish to improve his own character by eradicating a bad habit. He may do this by thinking carefully about it, by analysing the causes of the habit, by giving himself auto-suggestion in opposition to the habit. All this, even if the habit may not in the end be eradicated must be classed as directive thinking. *Directive thinking is thus obviously, controlled thinking requiring an effort of attention and concentration as opposed to phantasy thinking which knows but little control save that of desire, and little effort or concentration.*

In all the business of everyday life, directive thinking must be employed; whether we are merely using our minds to decide the most trivial problem, such as the best way of eradicating weeds from the garden, or whether we are deciding upon a policy to be pursued in some great commercial or political enterprise. Every time we use our brains in directive thinking we are establishing a habit which gradually gives us power to produce changes in our environment and in the world in general. Every time we indulge in phantasy thinking we encourage the habit of living in a world of our own ideas, and we are destroying the habit which enables us to create in reality.

The two forms of thinking may, of course, overlap considerably. The novelist or playwright, for instance, is very largely a phantasy thinker. He may feel the emotions of the various phantasy characters which he evolves, but in order to arrange the words and sentences, and furthermore in having an idea to portray or in drawing attention to evils which he thinks should be remedied, he is using considerable energy in directive thought. So that it becomes obvious that directive thought need not merely apply to the things of the immediate present nor even the near future, and in trying to draw distinction between the two, one is often confronted with a superficial criticism, that certain ideas must pertain to phantasy thinking, because they can never come to pass. That, however, is quite incorrect. The possibility that an idea may come to fruition in two or three hundred years time, and that the thoughts which have been given to the idea must assist its growth and ripening, is sufficient to constitute these thoughts as directive.

We must now look at the second important element in the child's early education, which would follow logically upon the first one that it should be made to face the facts around it; and that is, that in its games and occupations it should be encouraged, as far as possible, to take lines of directive thought, and not obtain its pleasures through phantasies only.

Thus, it would be much better to give him bricks to play with, so that he may use directive thought in designing and building a house, than to give him a ready-made toy, such as an engine wherewith he will merely carry out the phantasy of being a driver or a passenger and of travelling wheresoever he wishes. A toy wheel-barrow which he can take into the garden and fill with real stones and earth is far better than a doll which he will merely imagine to be something to be brought up like himself, which he will endow with phantastic life and feelings which are quite unreal. In fact, as far as possible, the child's games and occupations should involve his *doing* something, rather than merely imagining something. Of course, imagination and phantasy will come into its games, and are bound to do so, but as much directive thought as possible should be added.

The ordinary fairy-tale should be swept from the nursery; here the child does nothing but identify himself with the hero or heroine in the most impossible of situations of a purely phantastic type. There is plenty of scope for giving a child an interest in stories from the fairy-land of science, or from the lives of famous persons in the centuries that have passed; all of which, if properly selected and dressed up, will assist the child's directive thought. For though the facts with which the stories may deal are as wonderful as any of Grimm's fairy-tales, *they are facts of which the child will never have to be undeceived, and he will never have to have his faith shaken in the stories which he has learnt*; thus the child will learn from the outset to think directively.

I know that many mothers, when they read this, will be inclined to shake their heads and say to themselves, "Poor little darling, I could never treat it so." And that they will be inclined, as is shown very early in this book, to say "These things cannot be true," for they are not the ideas they are accustomed to. Yet I can assure them that by means of carrying out many of those actions and teachings which they think are pleasant and harmless, they are really damning the child, while many of these ideas which they might term cruel are really of the greatest value and kindness to it. Moreover, experience has shown that if diplomacy be used, the child will be as equally interested in wonderful facts as in wonderful phantasies. The only difference is that it is more trouble to the parent or educator to search out and deal with facts himself. It is quite true that the child's imagination requires training, as part of its intellectual education. But there is vast difference between encouraging it to imagine the possibility of impossible things, and encouraging it to exercise its imagination in realisation of facts, however far they may be removed from the experience of everyday life. Many people have the idea that a child should be encouraged to use its imagination; whereas in fact the child's imagination requires curbing, training, sublimating. Such people do not realise that the early life of a child is lived almost entirely in imagination, that it has no difficulty whatsoever in using its imagination, and that the real difficulty is in preventing it from using too much imagination directed into false channels and by-paths of permanent unreality.

Chapter 7. Identification

We must now traverse another path through which Narcissism wanders. We have emphasised the fact that when a child comes into the world, he is to himself the only real thing; the rest of the world is merely seen from his phantastic view point, and at this stage he accepts himself as the one all-powerful centre of everything. Another important fact which arises from this, however, we have not dealt with, and that is, that he does not separate the outer world from himself as a separate entity. His unconscious view point is that the world is subordinate to himself, beneath his omnipotent control, if you like, that it is a dream of his own imagining, that it is something which belongs to him in every sense of the word. This, summed up, means that it is part of himself, that his identity and the identity of the dream-world around him are part of the same thing.

Thus, the infant does not at first distinguish between himself and his mother. When he is hungry, he cries, and he probably has almost as ready access to his mother's breasts as if they were part of his own body. And such imagination is more than encouraged when he is allowed the use of a rubber teat to suck in the intervals between his meals.

It is generally a comparatively slow process through which the infant passes, this one of separating himself in thought and feeling from objects surrounding him. It is one which is hardly ever completely accomplished. We have already mentioned the fairy-tale which encourages the child's phantasy thought. Let us now see how he really obtains pleasure from that fairy-tale. It is by identification. In imagination he is a fairy prince or princess, as the case may be; his pleasure in the triumphs and progress of the central figure of the story is that of performing his prodigious deeds by proxy; and if he thus identifies himself with the hero of the story, he is also encouraged to believe that he possesses the power and qualities of that hero. He is less able to realise that he, unlike the hero, cannot perform magic deeds with a mere wave of a wand. Indeed, when the story is over, he will probably play at being a fairy, and in phantasy perform the magic deeds again.

This demonstrates the force of his identification with the hero of the story. *And it must be remembered that sooner or later the child will have to wake up, will have to realise that it possesses no magic power, and the struggle within it will be great.* It is obviously a mistaken form of kindness to enhance such pleasures of the moment, when you are merely accentuating the struggle which the child will have to make at a later period to overcome his Narcissism. In passing, I may mention that you have probably already done the child considerable damage by allowing him to have his rubber teat at the beginning of this period of identification, since he identifies it with the mother's breast, and is thus encouraged to think that the breast is always with him.

Let us now see where this Narcissistic identification may come out later in life.

First of all, it is this which enables us to enjoy novels, just as we enjoyed fairy-tales as children. We identify ourselves with the hero or heroine of the book, and in phantasy perform their various wonderful feats. Thus we satisfy our Narcissistic desire to be great and powerful. If we lack cleverness, and the hero is clever, by identification and imputation we may attain the pleasures of feeling clever and superior. If the heroine is beautiful and everyone falls in love with her, we may by proxy be the same. If the hero is a sailor, and we have always desired to sail, yet have never been on the sea, our ambition is now attained—and see how easily attained—in a truly omnipotent fashion, without effort on our part, just by reading about it. Exactly the same thing takes place at theatres, where the Narcissist identifies himself with the actors on the stage. So far so good; if a person can content himself with an occasional theatre or occasional novel, wherewith to take a restful regression to an infantile outlet of energy, no harm is done. There are times when we must rest, and there are times when we must sleep, which also appears to be Narcissistic regression to a condition somewhat resembling our pre-birth state. But there are many who cannot control their identification in this way, who cannot confine it to the stage and the novel, who bring it into the affairs of life continuously. They may unconsciously identify themselves with their father or mother, their relations or friends, or even their enemies, and perhaps, in turn, with everyone with whom they come into contact. Like a looking-glass, they reflect everything that goes on around them. They feel the pleasures of their friends, they also feel their pains. They are called sympathetic, they are often ultra-sympathetic—they are a nuisance.

I remember on one occasion I had asked a woman of strong Narcissistic temperament to take a fly out of the corner of my eye. She absolutely refused to do so under any consideration, as she was sure she would hurt me too much. Inquiry showed that Narcissism had exaggerated her own feelings, so that a speck of dust in her own eye was torture. Yet her eye was so tender and important to herself that she could not bear anyone to touch it even in order to get something out. *And she could not imagine that anybody else could have feelings that differed from hers*; and since she identified herself so much with other people, I have no doubt it would have been a real agony to her, had she attempted to extract the fly from my eye.

Such people are by no means uncommon. We all know the person who cannot bear to hurt us, even for our good. For instance, some cannot bear to bandage a wound for us since they cannot bear to see pain in any form. They state that it is almost as if they felt it themselves, and they call themselves "sympathetic." But in spite of popular belief to the contrary, such sympathy is not a virtue, there is nothing altruistic about it; it is an inconvenient fault of an entirely selfish kind. In order to help one's friend, one does not need to feel his feelings and suffer his pains, one wants to understand them; the more one enters into his feelings, the more one's judgment is biased, and the less one is able, as a rule, to be of assistance. Worse still, in connection with these people, they not only pour out sympathy in this way, but attribute it to themselves as a virtue, and they cannot bring themselves to believe their friends to be really good, unless their friends also can react in a similar way towards them. They call a normal person unsympathetic, perhaps exaggerate the term and call him brutal, wishing indeed that their friends who have climbed higher from Narcissism should regress to their lower stand-point.

I have given here but one type of Narcissistic identification with other persons; it seems to me unnecessary to carry it further since any reader who chooses to think the matter out for himself will find endless modifications of such identifications. We all possess it in part, and on the whole women are more Narcissistic than men. Let it not be thought, however, that this is a reflection on women; it is a reflection on the way they have been brought up, for from the earliest times environment impresses them with the idea that "little boys are made of slugs and snails and puppy-dogs' tails, and little girls are made of sugar and spice and all things nice!" And hence on such lines as these, their Narcissism is encouraged, and their capabilities of facing fact and reality discouraged from the very outset, until differences of temperament are produced in the adults of the two sexes, which in no way belong to Nature, but purely to our conventional and somewhat barbaric stand-point.

There are yet more important results of Narcissistic identification than those already mentioned; Narcissism leads, in many instances, to the choice of a particular love-object. Narcissism is, of course, by no means the only or chief factor in the choice of love-objects, as anyone who has studied psycho-analysis will at once realise. It is, however, the only one I intend to touch on in this particular work.

Just as the mythical Narcissus himself fell in love with his reflection, so does his prototype of to-day. An infant is not only the omnipotent centre of all, he is also the only interesting portion of the universe in his early days. His interests are entirely self-centred, and his joys and pleasures belong to himself alone; and as he grows older, everything that is like him is identified with himself. In the worst form of Narcissism in the adult, the individual remains entirely selfish, and is incapable of loving anybody outside himself at all.

By identification, however, he can love in a sense those attributes of his own personality which he sees in other persons. Thus, he may love somebody for a facial similarity, for a voice which is like his, or for tastes which are like his own, but most commonly he loves them for a body like his own. And from this we see that he may fall in love with somebody of his own sex. Hence, homo-sexuality,[5] as it is called, is frequently one of the distressing results of an early Narcissistic upbringing. But it need not be necessary for such homo-sexuality to be of a grossly erotic type; such desires may be for the most part repressed in the unconscious, or appear only in minor ways such as the desire to kiss, fondle or touch favoured persons of the same sex. On the other hand, frequently the early education and environment of the Narcissistic person has been such as to leave him quite incapable of complete repression; and we then have expressed more or less open erotic desires and actions for persons of the same sex. Such persons, however, should not be treated as criminals in this particular matter; they are by this time as hopelessly incompetent to deal with themselves, as is the kleptomaniac or a person having any other form of so-called degenerate mentality. Here again, we see the reason why homo-sexuality is so much more rife amongst women than amongst men. The minor details of their early environment tend so much more to confirm them in Narcissism. It is partially repressed and partially displaced homo-sexuality which causes some women to kiss one another, to call one another by affectionate names and so forth, to delight in taking hold of one another's hands on occasion; actions which normally, between persons of opposite sex, would at once be taken to indicate some sort of erotic affection, but which we are so used to seeing amongst women that we do not realise their repressed and unconscious significance.

Let it not be thought, however, that this subject of homo-sexuality is based on this one simple problem; there are many other early infantile fixations, which play a very large part in causing persons to become homo-sexual. I only mention this one Narcissistic complex as being another example of how identification takes place as one of the chief results of the Narcissistic temperament, and to what lengths such identification may, on occasion, lead. Of course, all degrees of such identifications may be met with, and it is quite common to find persons who can love hetero-sexually as well as homo-sexually; that is to say, who can love persons of the opposite sex in the

[5] Homo-sexuality—sensual love for a person of the same sex as oneself.

usual way, as well as persons of their own sex. But such people, even in their hetero-sexual love, tend to choose a love-object which resembles themselves in some manner or the other. However, a certain amount of Narcissism (which fortunately everyone still possesses), may be of value in this way, for it is certainly good for a man and woman to have similar interests when they marry; it is excessive Narcissism, excessive identification, excessive sympathy, which is deleterious, just as in other manifestations of Narcissism, with which we are going to deal shortly, it is excessive impatience, excessive anger, excessive tears which are really harmful, and lead to the greatest unhappiness. Although perhaps in these latter instances, to be without impatience, anger, or tears would be better still.

Thirdly, there is yet another method of Narcissistic identification. Just as a child identifies itself with its living surroundings, so does it identify itself with its inanimate surroundings. As its mother and nurse are treated as part of it in the early stages, so also are its rubber teat, feeding bottle and toys treated. If you take away the baby's rattle, it will cry or stamp or weep with as much vigour and display of emotion as if you had caused it bodily pain by means of rigorous physical punishment. You have in fact taken away part of itself from the little omnipotent person. In later stages in his career, if his Narcissism has been allowed to remain, the adult will still identify himself with his belongings. He will be absurdly upset at the breaking of a tea-cup which belongs to him, at the theft of some jewelry, at damage done to his clothing or property in some way, however trifling. He cannot realise that these things which belong to him are more or less unimportant trifles, which can be replaced, or if they cannot be replaced, can be equally well done without, if he has attained that philosophical attitude of mind which belongs to the person who has thrown off this uncomfortable spirit of Narcissistic identification. Moreover, the Narcissist who thinks himself to be the best and most important of beings, will attach similar importance to his property. If he drives an inferior motor-car, which breaks down on every journey he makes, he will excuse it in all sorts of irrational ways, he will praise it on every possible occasion as "the best car on the market," and what seems more absurd still, he will very likely think it the best car on the market. It is the same with his house, his books, with his relations, with everything that is even distantly connected with him. He will speak in high praise of them all, and be anxious, at all times, to show them off, and to uphold their virtues to all comers. The Narcissist, indeed, rationalises about things in general considerably more than most people. The fuller meaning of rationalization and its methods of working, however, we shall leave till later on.

Chapter 8. The Irritable Temperament

Irritability is not merely that quality in a person which makes his friends carefully guard their every word, lest inadvertently they should cause an outburst of temper, in its fullest sense it means over-sensitiveness to unpleasant stimuli, followed by over-reaction of any kind whatsoever. Thus, if a person by accident damage his clothing, his over-sensitiveness and over-reaction might result in an oath, in abusing the nail which tore his clothing or in abusing the workman who put the nail in place originally. It might again result in a feeling of depression, with anger displaced on to anyone who was present during the next hour, on the smallest pretext; or in an over-sensitive woman, it might result in an outburst of tears, or perhaps merely in volubly deploring the accident for half-an-hour with the next visitor who called; or she might merely "worry" about it, and keep turning the memory of it over and over in her mind, refusing to allow the fact to separate itself from her fancy.

All these various results, with many others which may be imagined, can be gathered together under the one term "irritability," or the term "over-sensitiveness" would do equally well. This irritability or over-sensitiveness may apply to material things or to purely mental ones. Narcissism may lead to an irritability of the body, and again it may lead to irritability merely of the mind. When Narcissism leads to an extremely sensitive body, it reacts to pain of every sort, however mild, as though it were acute. The omnipotent mind cannot bear to have its body disturbed. I gave an example a short while back of the lady who could not take a fly out of my eye, because her own eyes were so sensitive. Not only was this particular lady sensitive as regards her eyes, but at that period she was as afraid of the dentist touching a tooth as if it had been a serious abdominal operation. Pain of any sort or even slight accidents involving practically no pain, were reacted to as though they had been overwhelming misfortunes. Here we had an excellent example of one in whom Narcissism had produced extreme irritability of a physical nature.[6]

On the other hand, one finds a mental sensitivity equally pronounced. People who are always in fear lest somebody should find fault with them, with their mode of behaviour, with their manner of dress, even with their habit of thought. Unconsciously, to themselves they are the acme of perfection, they are the centre of importance, and they are inclined to think that people are paying very much more attention to them than is actually the case. They may consciously realise that they are not important at all, that other people do not give them a thought; but their unconscious Narcissism will not accept this slight upon their importance, and they remain miserably self-conscious in all their acts, reacting with exaggerated feeling whenever some slight criticism of their thoughts and actions appear even to be implied.

Pride, vanity, and self importance are other manifestations of this temperament. The person who feels slighted, or whose feelings are hurt when other persons think too little of his opinions, or pay too little attention to his actions, or, in fact, whose feelings are

---

[6] It may be of interest to readers to know that this physical over-sensitiveness has very largely disappeared from this particular lady as the result of partial psycho-analysis.

hurt easily by anything whatsoever, is for the most part a Narcissist, in whom once again the infantile omnipotence has been disturbed.

Jealousy very often represents the Narcissistic idea. The "dog-in-the-manger" attitude, which finding it cannot possess for itself, cannot bear anybody else to possess, is largely the attitude of unconscious phantasy, in which the individual cannot relinquish the idea that somehow he will succeed by means of his omnipotent mind in possessing the desired object, and his unconscious mind retains this idea so long as the object has not become the property of somebody else in such a definite and irrefutable manner as to prove in spite of his unconscious phantasy that he cannot possibly possess it himself.

The "dog-in-the-manger" attitude is one which simply refuses to recognise the impossibility of possessing something, although the desire for possession in any particular case may unconsciously mean nothing except the desire to prove to oneself one's own omnipotence. And many a case of jealousy in love-affairs is nothing but this unconscious desire to prove to oneself the possession of power; it is the hatred of acknowledging the fact that one has not control where one desires to have it most. Curious as it may seem jealousy is bred mostly out of self-love rather than out of love for the other person, although, of course, except in extreme cases, love for the other person may also exist.

The reaction which takes place whenever the Narcissistic element is hurt, almost always takes the form of a regression. It will be remembered that a regression implies a return to an infantile method of expression. The Narcissist unfailingly hopes, in his unconscious that his omnipotence will enable him to avoid an unpleasant fact, and to controvert it magically. He therefore falls back on those acts of infancy, which he found useful at that early period of his life as magical means of attaining his ends. Let us assume, for example, that our Narcissist has entered quietly into an argument with a friend, with full faith in himself and his argument that he will convert his friend to his own point of view. He finds, however, that he is getting the worst of the argument. This is unbelievable to him, he cannot realise it; his friend must be pig-headed. Rapidly his unconscious mind says to itself, "What methods did I employ in my childhood, what magic formula did I use then to obtain what I wished?" "Ah!" says the unconscious, "I remember; I used abusive terms to my nurse, and the dear thing did what I wanted at once." Very soon he is using abusive terms to his friend, who, however does not later on remark, "Oh! that man is a Narcissist." He merely says, "You know, So-and-So never can keep his temper in an argument." And the poor Narcissist all the time feels and thinks that he has been hardly dealt with, that people do not understand him, that they deliberately will not follow his arguments.

Of course, the last is very likely to be right, for in argument there is generally more rationalization than there is about most things in life. Nevertheless, the fact remains that it is not really important that his friend should understand either him or his argument as a rule, and if he were not Narcissistic he would not over-react to this stimulus.

Other methods of reaction in a like manner are all regressions to infancy. Some Narcissists, when they ask their unconscious memory, "What magic did I employ as a child?" find that it was the magic of words, and they use expletives of various kinds, which correspond in every way to the magic words which a conjuror whispers over his tricks when he performs the apparently impossible. Others remember in their unconscious mind that they wept copiously, that when they wept the feeding bottle was returned to their lips, or the toy to their hands. Others go back a stage further. They withdraw in to themselves, they refuse to speak, or they say, "I am so upset, I must go and lie down." They attempt to return, in fact, to the condition of isolation and rest, if not of pre-birth, at least of that period immediately following birth, when if they cried, they were rocked and crooned over and put to sleep.

Another form of regression largely due to Narcissism is that of alcoholism. Here again, there are other causes at work in the unconscious, but Narcissism is one of the most important of them. The Narcissist does not like real responsibility; he certainly thinks that he is always desiring responsible posts and positions, but this is merely because to hold a responsible position or to have responsibility signifies importance and power. As a matter of fact, when responsibility is thrust upon him, he often has a strong tendency to avoid it, because responsibility entails dealing with facts as they are, and not with phantasies; and the responsibility which the Narcissist seeks is largely that of phantasy. In spite, therefore, of his statements to the contrary, we know that he wishes to run away from responsible positions, and alcohol has a peculiar power of enabling one to forget the responsibilities of the moment, and at the same time to give one a feeling of potency and well-being. Consequently, when the Narcissist comes up against an unpleasant fact, a responsibility which he does not wish to take, anything in fact which disturbs his sense of well-being, alcohol serves the purpose of allowing regression to infancy. It returns him very swiftly to that early period when he had no responsibility, when he need take no thought of the facts around him, when he had a sense of well-being and omnipotence. This potency is increased by the fact that it also removes, simultaneously, other repressions, that is, it allows other forms of infantile energy to be expressed without conscious criticism or hindrance.

Exactly the same thing may be said of drug-taking. The drug-taker is simply habitually seeking something to remove his responsibilities, to lead him away from his conflicts which he does not wish to face, away from the world of reality into an infantile world, where whatever his surroundings, whatever the facts that exist, he is able to ignore them, and feel himself in phantasy their master.

But the curious thing about all these regressions is that, in a sense, they serve to satisfy the individual. They comfort him with the unconscious assurance at the moment they are performed, that all will, somehow, be well, that these reactions will somehow bring about the desired end, that the abuse will succeed where the argument did not, that the tears will somehow perform their magic act, that a rest in bed will bring about new life, and that the new life will succeed where the old life failed.

Never does the Narcissist realise facts as they are, deal with them as facts, see them in their proper proportions, and leave them alone when he cannot use them.

Impatience of a different kind is also one of the common reactions. A man may go into a restaurant; he finds it is full, and quite naturally he is kept waiting a few minutes before the busy waiter can bring him the menu. He refuses to recognise the fact that he is only one of a hundred persons present, that the restaurant has to be run at a profit to the proprietor, that innumerable waiters cannot therefore be kept to serve his high omnipotence; he frets with impatience and he cannot resign himself to the inevitable waiting. He will not understand that *time* is one of the factors over which he has no power. In fact, this difficulty to realise the *factor of time* is an extremely common one with Narcissists. No sooner has a project entered their heads than they expect to see it fulfilled. Such fulfilment can only take place in phantasy, just as they did indeed attain their wishes in childhood. As children they could instantaneously create a chariot and horses from an arm-chair with complete neglect of the time-factor, and now as adults, they hope instantaneously to create an omelet without waiting for it to be cooked, to create a business or a character, or fame or happiness in the same instantaneous way, without reference to time. They are quite unable to see, completely and wholly, any difference between the phantasy of childhood and facts of adult life; and one of the most essential differences between the two is this *time factor*.

It takes minutes for an omelet to be cooked, it takes years for a business to be created, it takes a lifetime for a character to be formed, fame they may never attain, but happiness lies within their grasp at once, if only they could relinquish their Narcissism.

Chapter 9. Rationalization

Having now briefly sketched the birth and some of the possible developments of Narcissism, it may be well to revert to the subject of rationalization, on which I have already touched briefly, before I deal with some of the methods with which we may combat our Narcissistic tendencies. The reason for reverting here to rationalization is this. Already I know that there are few readers who will not have discovered some material in this book which will have touched a tender spot in themselves. And since we know that the great effort of Narcissism is to cover up those tender spots, and to deceive ourselves in thinking that either they are not there, or better still, that they are virtues and really particularly healthy spots, it is as well to examine these tendencies and observe one of the chief methods by which we do produce such disguises successfully. Of these methods of disguise, our greatest comforter, yet our worst enemy, is rationalization. The term means *"finding apparently adequate reasons for things."*

One of the qualities which we highly cultured animals possess is that of reason. We have discovered that logic is one of the essential factors of law and order, and that the highest form of intellect possesses reason in a large measure. Among our gods, the god of reason and logic stands high, and our very Narcissism will not permit us to do and accept things which are contrary to logical reasoning. For that means in the first place, that they are contrary to what we have been taught to revere highly as a good quality, and yet more still it means that they are contrary to the magic of WORDS, for logic means words; logic is words which follow one another in irrefutable sequence. And we have already learnt that *the infant has early associated words and sounds with magic, since by the persistent use of these he has got what he wanted*. So that doubly are logic and reason revered.

Now, the unhappy thing about life is that we are continually wishing to do things or feel things or believe things which do not follow logically upon other things which we have also had to feel or think or believe at some time. Some of our wishes are logically incompatible with other of our wishes. More over, we very often do not wish to believe or think things which do follow logically on actual facts which have gone before. How are we then, as reasonable people, to deal with the situation? By rationalization, by finding a reason which suits our purpose; and this can only be done, as a rule, by leaving out some important factor, by ignoring some truth, and by arguing from false premises. We do not do this consciously, that would be unworthy. Our unconscious censor manages to delete from consciousness the unpleasant truth, as we have already pointed out, and brings forth an array of facts which appear irrefutable, and he succeeds in giving us most plausible reasons so that we may believe that which is most convenient to us.

Let us consider for a moment such a subject as religion. The Roman Catholic will adduce evidences of various kinds to show that his is the only right and proper form of religion to be accepted by any intellectual person. The Baptist will likewise do the same, and will probably hold that Papal institutions, in many instances, spring not from Heaven but from Hell. If you discuss it with either of them, you may be flooded with reasons, logical evidences of the correctness of their views. Obviously, they cannot both be right in so exclusive a manner, and a very little insight will show that the reasons they adduce have really very little to do with their beliefs, although they think they have. Reverence for their parents, early environment, and other factors of this kind, have really induced their present beliefs, but these would not appear to them as logical reasons and so they select others.

So it is with any unpleasant theory which comes into being. At the time of Darwin, a large number of facts were discovered which led unbiassed persons to believe in the theory of evolution. This appeared contrary to many religious beliefs, and the general public did not want to accept such a theory. They could not, however, shut their eyes to facts; what were they to do? By carefully leaving out some of the facts, and introducing speculative material, which they called facts, but which were not facts, they succeeded in producing excellent reasons, or what seemed excellent reasons to them, for refuting the theory of evolution and retaining their old beliefs. In other words, they went through a process of rationalization.

The same thing was taking place a few years ago with reference to psycho-analysis. People did not like their omnipotent feelings disturbed, did not like to find that the superior bricks of which their edifice had been built were originally made from clay, and they found excellent reasons for not believing it. This, fortunately for progress, is gradually passing away, just as the opposition to the idea of the evolution of the body passed away. But rationalization is a process which has been and is still going on continuously. When Harvey discovered the circulation of the blood, when Galileo discovered that the earth went round the sun, when psycho-analysts discovered that much which mothers thought kind was really cruel, and when you read a book which tends to point out that some of your cherished virtues may possibly be faults, the same tendency is at work. Your mind sorts out some of the reasons, refuses to look at others of them, and by such careful selection, by this unconscious process of rationalization, supports your belief in yourself, holds fast to that which has been, and attempts continuously to prevent further changes and disturbances. This rationalization, however, is much more widely distributed than I have so far indicated; in order that one fact may be justified by reason, all the lesser facts which come before it must be similarly justified, until even into the trivial details of everyday life the leaven of rationalization has penetrated. Examples of it may be seen every day in the newspapers, in politics, in even trifling arguments. Take for instance the subject of woman's suffrage. One half of the country produced irrefutable arguments to prove how bad it was, the other half to prove how good it was. In both cases, the arguments were but straws in the wind, they were quite unnecessary, they were only rationalization. Long before the argument on either side came into being, the feelings were there, the desires were there; and desires must somehow be proved right with the magic of words, before we feel at liberty to fulfil them. In neither case in this argument was the root of the matter touched. If some philosopher had come forward and said, "The first question we have to ask before thinking about suffrage, is should a woman wear a skirt?" or some such similar fundamental question, it would probably have been said that it had nothing to do with matter, and yet this question of *artificial* difference between the sexes is really fundamental to the whole subject. But the rationalist will find that he will not meet me in this statement. The woman who wishes to retain certain privileges, and yet accept certain other privileges, will at once find reasons why she should wear a skirt and yet have the vote. She will tell me all sorts of things about her physical disabilities, things which she believes to be fundamental truths, many of which, in fact, are fundamentally wrong, but accepted as truths because they lead to rationalization being able to support her wishes.

In a similar way, on the much discussed subject of "prohibition" the prohibitionist will rationalise on a certain few facts, in order to support his emotions and desires. A moderate drinker will do exactly the same, in the opposite direction. Neither of them will have the courage to ignore his personal feelings, nor may he have the power to do so, and to take all the facts into consideration and come to a conclusion, irrespective of his wishes on the subject.[7]

Of course, one of the other difficulties in the way of coming to correct conclusions in all these things is that people will insist on arguing upon subjects, when the amount of real scientific knowledge they have on the subjects is extremely small. The newspaper editor will quote a few popular facts, in order to support some theory of his own, having but a limited knowledge of psychology, physiology, anatomy, or of some other science which has considerable bearing on the subject, he will end by producing a series of conclusions probably entirely wrong. This, of course, is inevitable in our limited circumstances; but it should not be equally inevitable that we should hold firmly to our beliefs, when we realise how limited is our knowledge of any one subject. And in order to examine facts and to get rid of rationalization as far as possible, we must try, with the utmost power at our command to refuse that reaction of self-defence and self-pride, which prevents us from looking at ourselves and from realising that most of our opinions about ourselves may be completely erroneous. We must be prepared to accept temporary, not fixed, judgments, based upon the evidence which we have. We must be prepared to reverse those judgments in the light of new evidence. We must be careful not to reject this evidence merely because we do not like it.

It will now be seen how very necessary it is, in dealing with Narcissism in particular, to understand something of rationalization, so that we may be on our guard in examining ourselves, against allowing this to play too great a part in our conclusions. Otherwise, with all the goodwill in the world, we may never succeed in making any improvement whatsoever, in ourselves. The greatest scientists themselves have been amongst those who realised this.

It was Darwin who wrote, as we have quoted in the earlier part of this book, "I had, during many years, followed a golden rule, namely, that whenever a published fact, a new observation or thought came across me, which was opposed to my general results, to make a memorandum of it without fail and at once, for I had found by experience that such facts and thoughts were far more apt to escape from the memory than favourable ones."

And it was the great scientist, Helmholtz, who said, "It is better to be in actual doubt, than to rock oneself in dogmatic ignorance."

---

[7] Of course this does not imply that no one is ever capable of putting his conscious feelings on one side, and examining a subject in spite of pre-conceived ideas and desires, but that this is the exception rather than the rule.

PART 2. PRACTICAL APPLICATIONS

Chapter 10. Self Analysis

In attempting to cure ourselves of hyper-Narcissistic characteristics, there are several lines of treatment which may be followed, some of which depend upon the particular manifestation of Narcissism with which we have to deal. One, however, which should be followed in every case, we borrow from the methods of psycho-analysis. We cannot call it psycho-analysis because the technique employed by an amateur in examining himself must be vastly different from the technique employed by a psycho-analyst in dealing with his patient. But it is a modification of one detail of the technique of psycho-analysis which, if properly applied, may have far-reaching results. It is on the lines of that phenomenon which is known generally as ab-reaction, and is as follows.

When an individual has come to the conclusion that he is suffering from some characteristic of Narcissistic nature, which he would rather be without, he should, first of all, carefully call to mind, and if possible make historical notes of the situations which stimulate the particular temperamental reaction to which he objects. If he can, he should go further than this, and recall as many as possible of the actual situations of recent date, when this particular reaction has been called forth.

If he have an ungovernable temper, for example, he should, in detail, go first into the type of situations which call forth that temper, and secondly, he should revise in detail the recent occasions upon which he has lost his temper, and thirdly, *he should attempt to find out the particular moment, the particular words, the particular occasion which first began to stir feelings of temper within him before he actually began to show violent manifestations of it.*

Having all these things set forth satisfactorily, it would be well if he spent half-an-hour every day, for a considerable period, in performing the next part of the treatment. He should go into a room by himself, where he will not be disturbed, recline on a couch or a comfortable chair, and allow his mind to drift backwards, year by year, remembering as far as possible, every instance on which the unfavourable symptom has been called forth. He will find that if he does not concentrate too hard, but merely keeps in mind the various causes of his temper and recent manifestations of it, other times and instances will come into his mind unbidden. He will, in fact, be surprised at the amount of detail which he can remember concerning the matter. Things which he had not thought of for years, happenings which he had passed over as trivial, will come into his mind, and be found to have stimulated, in some way or the other, the ill-temper (or other Narcissistic trouble) which he is endeavouring to get rid of. He must take himself, as far as possible, right into childhood. He will not necessarily of course, go back as far as this on the first few occasions, but after he has been at work on himself in this way for some days, he should have no trouble whatever in beginning to recall some of the infantile occasions upon which his Narcissism called forth temper.

In all the instances which he brings up into his conscious mind, he should write down and study not only the facts remembered, but also the emotions which he felt. These he should examine from every possible point of view, and see what Narcissistic element appears to be present in them. Many memories will come into his mind of an infantile nature which do not express the particular symptom from which he now suffers, but will obviously have some bearing on it. These he should examine in the same way, because it is important for him to get into his conscious mind as much as possible of the various occasions in his life on which Narcissism acted, when he was not conscious of it. Not only must he see how these various occasions were exhibitions of Narcissism, but he must try and trace them back, and must compare them with his typical infantile methods of expression. These may be represented by shouting, crying, stamping, weeping or any other infantile manifestations of those omnipotent phantasies which now seem to him to be the starting-point of his more recent expression of them. He has, in fact, to lay bare before himself, as much as possible of his previously unconscious Narcissistic life; its beginnings, its evolution, and its ultimate form. This making conscious of what was previously unconscious or but partly conscious, is, in itself, a most potent factor in improvement, if he will have the patience to steadily persevere and to go over daily, for a considerable period, the material he has brought to the surface. If he does not do this regularly, it is liable to sink back, and become once again an unconscious factor and a determinant to his actions over which he has no control.

This bringing into consciousness the unconscious causes and motives under-lying behaviour is, in psycho-analysis, one of the powerful factors at work producing cures of neurotic obsessions and so forth, and it is equally potent with the minor temperamental abnormalities with which we are dealing here. For it means that previous mental conflicts which were either wholly or partially unconscious, are now rendered conscious habitually; and a conscious conflict, or rather a conflict in which the forces at work become conscious, is far easier to direct than one in which the very forces themselves are hidden and unknown. Let us take a more material example for comparison. Suppose an officer to be in command of a company of soldiers out in the desert, and attacked on a dark night by savages. It might very well be that he was well armed, that his machine guns were efficient, but that he would be quite overwhelmed because he could neither see the savages nor know their numbers, their whereabouts nor their armaments. But supposing that the War Office had thoughtfully equipped him with one or two good search-lights, which he could direct upon the savages so that the number of savages, their armaments, position, and so forth, could be brought into his consciousness, he would be in a far better position, for he could direct his machine-guns at the threatened points, instead of being forced to fire them wildly and as likely as not miss his targets altogether.

Exactly the same happens with these manifold feelings to which I have just been referring. The more one can see of them, their histories, their evolution, their beginnings, the more one holds them in consciousness, the easier does the conflict between good and evil become in the individual. Again, this method of self-help which I have given here, differs considerably from that pursued in psycho-analysis, in that it is following up only one unconscious factor, albeit, one of the most important factors; but in psycho-analysis we follow up in turn all the unconscious forces at work, great and small, and in any temperamental abnormality there are certainly many more unconscious factors than Narcissism concerned, although Narcissism may be the predominant one. Thus, for instance, alcoholism, though always possessing a Narcissistic element, frequently has other determinants present of an exceptionally strong[8] nature. So that while an analysis of Narcissism only, may be of the greatest value

---

[8] Alcoholism is further complicated by the fact that a habit of *physical* craving is formed, which as a rule cannot be overcome by mental treatment alone. This craving, fortunately, can now be eradicated by medicinal means. Indeed, patients of mine have been cured of all desire for alcohol in about one week as a

in some cases, in others, where Narcissism does not occupy so great a field, the other unconscious factors are too potent to allow much benefit to accrue from a partial self-analysis of this kind.

In drug-taking, however, there is a slight difference from alcoholism, for, as a rule, Narcissism is nearly always the essential factor. It will be understood that Narcissism links itself to almost any other characteristic, influencing it for the worse by fixing it more deeply, and holding it back from becoming conscious more strongly than would otherwise be the case.

The patient will find himself, during this self-examination, repeatedly trying to excuse himself. He will find himself saying, "I remember on such an such an occasion losing my temper, but on that occasion I was perfectly justified." Or in another instance, he may say, "I remember weeping (or I remember being depressed or angry, or impatient), but circumstances then existed which seem to me proper occasions for such a manifestation to have taken place."

Let me emphasise at the outset, that any such excuses will be rationalizing; that he must say to himself, "Whether they appear normal or abnormal, according to accepted standards, those occurrences most certainly had their Narcissistic factor."

For it must be understood that although there are many occasions when impatience or weeping may be looked upon, conventionally, as normal occurrences, that is only because everybody possesses certain imperfections due to Narcissism; and if one is going to attempt to improve one's temperament in this way, every occasion must be examined without excuse or rationalization, otherwise the individual who is thus at work upon himself will only succeed in defeating himself to his own detriment, by putting up a resistance to his cure or improvement.

And, indeed, one of the important factors in this work, just as in psycho-analysis itself, is the factor which comes into play in overcoming these resistances of seeing ourselves as we are, of seeing the evolution and beginnings of our temperament as it really was.

This is bound to reveal in all of us without exception much that is unpleasant, and that we would rather not see. Resistance to seeing such material is inevitable, if the

rule. The patient is then in somewhat the same condition as a man who has never tasted alcohol, and he will have no craving for alcohol thereafter, unless he deliberately drinks it again. Herein, however, we see the importance of the psychic factor, for should the cured alcoholic begin again to take alcohol, either because he thinks that he has attained self control and can do so, or because he finds abstinence difficult on social grounds, he will almost inevitably regress to his old condition of uncontrolled desire, no matter how long has elapsed since he was cured of it. *The same causes which originally led him to excess, viz., his mental complexes, are still present and again produce similar results.* Of course, a very large proportion of those who have been cured by medicinal treatment do not relapse, because they have sufficient common sense not to experiment with themselves. In the other cases, however, the only hope of a permanent cure consists in following up the physical treatment with mental treatment, i.e., analysis.

On the other hand, in most cases of drug taking a medicinal cure is generally sufficient, for there is no "social urge" to taking drugs as there is in the case of alcohol, and once the craving has been cured, the tendency to experiment again is the exception rather than the rule. But even here it is found that any indulgence in the drug, however slight, will again produce in the individual his old craving. *He has found a previous path of narcissistic regression and will inevitably follow it, for though the craving had been eradicated the complexes remain.* There are many potential alcoholics and potential drug-takers in the world, but they will never know it unless unfortunate chance induces them to open that particular channel of regression.

examination is sufficiently thorough. If no resistance has to be overcome, the individual may be certain that he is shirking the facts.

Chapter 11. Readjustment Of Objectives

In the last chapter we described a process of self-assistance of the kind which should be applied by any person, to any Narcissistic manifestation he may desire to improve. In the present chapter we are going to deal with a method of treatment which is by no means necessary in all cases, but is very necessary in a large proportion of them.

We must bear in mind that the Narcissist's inability to realise distinctly the difference between phantasy and fact will often lead him to suppose possible that which is impossible in the ordinary affairs of everyday life, and to ignore difficulties which may really be insuperable, which stand in the way of his aims and projects. He will thus be continually finding himself at a disadvantage, continually failing, from apparently trivial reasons, to accomplish an end, and as a result he may become depressed, nervous, worried, and subject to that lassitude accompanied by headaches, which so frequently comes to the Narcissist when he struggles unavailingly with the ordinary aims and tasks of everyday life. Moreover, not only does he fail to recognise the difficulties in the way of any particular task, but he fails to recognise the fact that two projects which he has in his mind may be incompatible with one another; or he fails to recognise that great *"Time-factor,"* which I have mentioned before, and tries to condense more work and more visible results into a given period than is humanly possible.

This type of Narcissist is always considerably addicted to day-dreams, with which, however, we shall deal in a further chapter. For the present, we are going to restrict ourselves to the question of arranging his aims and wishes on a sound and possible basis. In the first place, let it be understood that although the method of treatment so far carried out may have made clear to the patient the origin and development of his phantasy thought and phantastic aims, there yet remains the breaking of the habit, and this is rendered far more easy if we attempt to substitute another habit of a different nature. Let us further impress upon him the fact that a frequent examination of his aims in a directive manner by the method about to be discussed is in itself an exercise in directive thinking, helping to form a habit opposed to a former habit of phantasy thinking. And, lastly, let it be remembered that Narcissists are generally very averse from making real personal sacrifices which have no glamour attached to them; that they object to adapting themselves to reality which may be unpleasant, and that by the method I am about to describe, they will have to deal in trivial things, and the conscious adjustment which they will thus make towards reality will gradually become habitual.

What we are attempting to do now is to substitute directive thought and directive aims, aims possible of attainment, for phantasy thoughts and impossible aims. Most people will find on self-examination that their aims are by no means clearly defined; they have an object in life, but it is vague in outline, and ill-defined; it is often only a question of getting somehow through life, with enough food to eat, and sufficient phantasy thought to keep them from boredom. This again, is especially the case with some women, whose household duties require but little directive thought, since they are daily repetitions of the same thing. Dusting a room is a habit which becomes pleasanter if accompanied by phantasy thinking; whereas, had that woman some definite aim, apart from the habit of house-cleaning, it would be possible to accompany the room-dusting with directive thought which revolved round the aim in question, and this would very much add to the pleasure and efficiency of the individual's life. If a person, on self-examination, finds that his aims are not clearly defined, or are in conflict with one another, or, on the other hand, that his aims or thoughts are in part phantasy and impossible of fulfilment, that person should at once deliberately remould and re-state his aims, so that they become:

(a) clearly defined,

(b) clearly possible.

Moreover, the aims should be of two kinds:

(1) immediate,

(2) remote.

The remote aim is the ideal for which he is striving; and however high that ideal be, it should be of a kind possible of fulfilment, not necessarily in the lifetime of the individual, in all cases, for he may be working for something of which he does not expect fulfilment for even hundreds of years, yet it may be perfectly legitimately termed a real aim, as opposed to a phantastic one.

Now, the first thing which the individual should bear in mind is that an immediate aim should always be in harmony with the remote aim. Let it also be borne in mind that when we state that the aim should be clearly possible, we do not only mean that the aims should be possible from a point of view of external environment and circumstances, but also having regard to the patient's own intelligence, will-power, education, and physical health—in other words possible in the case of this particular individual.

Now let us consider in detail the further course to be pursued by the person who proposes to treat himself on these lines. Let him take pencil and paper and write out in the fullest of details a list of his aims, great and small, in the first place, without any reference to their bearing upon one another, or any attempt at classification, keeping in mind that by aims in life, we mean wishes which he hopes will be fulfilled. Let him think of every conceivable wish in his mind, and write it down, whether phantastic in nature, or trivial, or whether both possible and important.

In the next place, let him see that this list is written so clearly and accurately, that each of the aims is well defined and without ambiguity. Now let him run through the list again, and see whether any of the aims are in conflict with one another, and whether any of them are inconsistent from the view point of his, and are therefore impossible of fulfilment. Let him put his pencil definitely through such impossible aims, and cut them out of his life, with as full a realisation as possible of the fact that they are nothing but dreams, that he need never consider them again, that he must not regret them, for that is mere infantile crying after the impossible. He must replace them in due course with others possible of fulfilment.

Now let him take the revised list and separate it into two divisions, writing the aims down again under the two headings, (1) immediate aims, and (2) remote aims. Here, he will have to bear in mind one of his chief faults, if he be strongly Narcissistic. Such persons in their phantasy carry their aims to completion long before reality can permit of it. The time-factor is not realised, and hence they have a great tendency to confuse remote aims with the immediate aims, in their desire to see immediate results; hence, also, because they cannot soon see such results, they give way to despair, become depressed, and have the tendency to regress to the infantile characteristics to which I have already referred. Here lies the importance of dividing the aims into immediate and remote. For as soon as the individual's mind has grasped the fact that an aim is necessarily remote, and therefore impossible of immediate fulfilment, he is much more able to adjust himself to these facts, and to pay real and undivided attention to the immediate present. Apart from the fact that sorting and adjusting of the aims relieves the mind of many previous conflicts, it acts as a stimulus to a considerable amount of directive thinking. And the patient will be surprised at first to find the amount of time it is possible to spend in a really useful recasting of his life interests.

It was not until the author, himself, took pencil and paper, and classified his own aims, and put down the points for and against each, and attempted to see the disharmonies existing amongst them, that he realised the full value of this procedure. It might be thought that in a very short period any person could put down all his aims, and that but little modification would take place in them from day to day. This, however, is very far from being true, as will be seen by anyone who carries out this method fully.

Perhaps at this point the details taken from a case of a woman suffering from a "nervous breakdown" in which I used this method as a subsidiary form of treatment, may not only be of interest, but will also throw some light on the practical working of the method. I may mention that her chief troubles were insomnia, constant worrying, great depression, and inability to settle down to work of any kind.

In the first place, this patient commenced by stating that she had no aim in life at all. She had to admit, however, immediately after, that she had at least the aim of wishing to get well, or otherwise she would not have come to me. On being asked why she wished to get well, several subsidiary aims appeared. For the most part, they were rationalization, and I knew these aims would be thrown over in due course, but that, for the purpose in view, did not matter. I told her to go home, and write down her aims, in the manner I have just indicated.

The following was the list brought to me on the next day.

(1) To be well.

(2) To be married.

(3) To become a doctor.

(4) And if I cannot do that, to become a masseuse.

(5) Or a psycho-analyst.

(6) Or a private secretary.

(7) And I should like to have two children.

With this rather pathetic list in front of me, I asked her to give as far as possible the reasons she had for these various wishes, and to examine these on the lines I had indicated, with the following results.

(1) *To get well.* "The reason for this aim is obvious; it is necessary in order to obtain the others," said she.

(2) *To get married.* "This aim has three subsidiary immediate aims," she replied, "and there may be others. (a) I want a comfortable home of my own, (b) I want satisfaction of my natural instincts in accordance with the custom of ordinary adult life, (c) I could attain the later aim of having two children." She immediately added, "In that case, the

aim of having two children is a remote aim, and if I follow your advice I must no longer have day-dreams about them, I must put them out of my thoughts, I must not waste time on anything connected with them, until I am married."

(3) *To become a doctor.* "Concerning this," she added, "I have always liked studying Zoology, and microscopic work, and diseases. Moreover, it is the only way in which one can make money in a really interesting manner." She then stated that she realised this to be a double aim, and to consist, firstly, of the aim of earning a livelihood, and secondly, of that of having an interesting occupation. This aim was soon discovered to be phantastic, however, for she had to admit that her financial position would not permit of the necessary study, and that there was no prospect of any improvement in this. She therefore realised that although she had had it at the back of her mind for several months that somehow such an aim might be possible of fulfilment, she now clearly saw that it was not. She at once removed it from the list, and realised that neither regrets nor phantasy in connection with it would be of any avail, and again, that she must bear in mind possibilities and realities.

(4) *To become a masseuse.* She at once stated her thoughts on this subject. "I have known one or two masseuses, who seem to make money, and who are very happy. Moreover, it is an occupation that a lady can take up." She then discovered that this involved three aims: (a) to make money, (b) to be happy, (c) to remain genteel. On the opposite side, however, she added that she was not sufficiently physically strong for the work, and was afraid she would soon tire of it, because as an occupation itself, it did not appeal to her. This aim, also, immediately disappeared from the list.

(5) *To become a psycho-analyst.* This, said she, was a very interesting subject, and she thought she could do much good by means of it. Moreover, she thought she would like psychology though she had not studied it much as yet. "Moreover," said she, "psycho-analysts probably make a lot of money. And further, it would be very nice to sit at home in an arm-chair to do one's work, and to let other people do the talking." She at once recognised this latter idea to be a thoroughly Narcissistic regression. And then she found that all the other ideas contained multiple aims in themselves, each of which had to be thought out and classified, and into the details of which I need not go. Except to say that when she considered the matter from a practical point of view, the difficulties of training, the time it would take, and more especially the fact that she feared that psycho-analysis might not be popular by the time she was ready, she determined that it was only a phantasy aim, upon which she had been wasting phantasy thought, and she ruled it out.

(6) *To become a private secretary.* On this point, she considered that her personal appearance and general education would help her, and was quite compatible with the aim. But she knew no shorthand, book-keeping, nor typewriting. She, however, realised at once that the immediate aim in this case should be the shorthand, book-keeping, and typewriting, and she said, "I will go to-morrow and see where I can learn these things." I pointed out to her that she might very possibly change her mind, when she considered things further, but that even if she did so, the mastery of shorthand, typewriting and book-keeping might stand her in good stead, and in any case that she would be working for an immediate object, in turning some of her phantasy into directive thought. And on the morrow, she actually did commence her studies on these subjects.

(7) *The desire to have two children.* This was at once classified, as I have already said, as a remote aim; though, as a matter of fact, she got married shortly afterwards, and the remote aim is now on the way to being fulfilled, as she has one child.

I have shown by this example the ill-considered, phantastic, and conflicting aims, which some persons may at first produce when they attempt deliberately to classify them. But it must be remembered that each of the subsidiary aims which she had discovered her primary aims to be divided into were, in turn, again capable of being divided into further subsidiary aims. And the next stage of this form of technique is to discover these. Day by day, the pencil and paper must be brought out, and a list of aims and wishes for that day compiled and considered. They must be in turn examined to show (1) whether they are compatible with one another, (2) whether they are compatible with other immediate aims, (3) whether they are compatible with the remote aims.

A strong attempt must then be made to eradicate any aims or wishes which are antagonistic to one another, or to the primary aims of the individual, which have already been passed as real. As progress is made, definite and personal aims will be developed day by day, many of these, no doubt, apparently trivial, others at least important for the day in question, all important from the point of view of developing the habit of thinking in terms of reality.

For instance, on one occasion, the lady above mentioned wrote on her list in the morning that she wished to work hard at her shorthand in the early part of the day, to go to a matinée in the afternoon, and to a dance in the evening. On consideration, however, she came to the conclusion that the dance in the evening, following after the day's work and entertainment, would probably interfere with her next morning's work, and it was not, moreover, compatible with that immediate aim of regaining complete health at the earliest possible moment. It was, therefore, rejected; the lesser aim was recast, and a quiet dinner with a friend substituted. Only by such rigorous and possibly painful self-treatment can the Narcissist's conflicts be regulated and viewed in a proper perspective.

Every daily aim has a further subsidiary aim appertaining to it. For instance, a man may have made up his mind to devote a certain part of the day to studying; the lesser aim includes the subject to be studied, the amount to be done, and the time to be occupied. It is important that he should not over-estimate the amount he can get done in a given time. One reason why so much detail should be considered, is that it is astounding how excessively a person, with a tendency to phantasy thought, over-estimates the amount of work it is possible to get through in a given time. No sooner is a task commenced than he expects it to be almost finished. The daily programme frequently includes far more than is possible, and he forms a habit of being late for everything; all this being merely the ordinary omnipotent idea of childhood, which fulfils a wish in phantasy as readily as it is formed.

I must now give a warning, that those who follow this method are, at first, nearly always extremely impatient for results, for this very reason that they do not realise the time-factor; and they must realise, and consciously and patiently accept inevitable delay, with the assurance that if they can overcome their Narcissism sufficiently to persist in the method they will steadily and gradually develop a habit, an attitude of mind which devotes its energy to directive thought, to real aims, and to displacing from themselves the phantastic medley which was there before.

Chapter 12. Readjustment Of Thought

We have seen in an earlier chapter how one of the ways in which Narcissism manifests itself is in day-dreams. We saw how a child would substitute a phantasy or day-dream for a reality, and so fulfil its wishes and desires in this unreal manner. And we saw how, if this were persisted in to excess, the same or a modified method of fulfilling one's wishes in realms of phantasy would remain even in adult life. I may here remark that even *very little* day-dreaming constitutes excess, and is bound to have a deleterious effect upon the efficiency and happiness of the individual's life; unless, perhaps, that individual is mixing sufficient directive thought with his phantasies as in the case of a novelist or artist, for instance. In realising this, it must be borne in mind, that time and energy spent in phantasy thinking are time and energy lost to reality and fact; that the encouragement of the habit of phantasy thinking destroys the ability to think directively, or rather renders the full development of it impossible. Moreover, by encouraging day-dreams, we are simultaneously holding on to our Narcissism, and making it more likely that it will also find outlets in other deleterious ways. For instance, the "worrying nature" which is constantly thinking of possible troubles to come, and of how past troubles might have been avoided is indulging in a form of phantasy thinking. If the habit of phantasy thinking has been cultivated for pleasurable purposes, a channel has been opened which will be used without conscious intention for other kinds of phantasy as well. The habit of worrying to which we have just referred, is an example of this.

Worry consists in weaving phantasies about something which cannot at the moment be influenced directively. It may be about something which *has* happened and therefore cannot be influenced at all by thinking about it, or about something which *may* happen but over which the thinker has no immediate control; and it consists in going over all the "mays" and "mights" connected with the case, and experiencing the unpleasant emotions belonging to each phantasied situation. In order to get rid of this worrying habit, to close the channel which permits of it, a person must simultaneously cut out pleasurable day-dreams also, and thus close the channel entirely. Therefore, let us recommend the individual who indulges largely in day-dreams, to get rid of the habit as soon as possible. Those who have other abnormal characteristics which they wish to eradicate, should understand that they must, simultaneously, get rid of their day-dreams. And this means pulling oneself up, not merely when one discovers oneself imagining some glorious vista in which one occupies a principle but impossible part, it means similarly pulling oneself up in a thousand little ways; it means catching oneself whenever one wanders from a type of directive thought to a type of phantastic thought.

For instance, in the examination of one's aims, one is thinking directively, and one comes to the conclusion that, say, a course of shorthand and typewriting shall be taken at once, that the aim of being a secretary is one suitable and compatible with one's attainments. At this point, it is very easy for the individual to suddenly find that he or she has become, in day-dreams, the secretary of a duke or American millionaire. And if he does not pull himself up at this stage, he will find that the duke's money has been left him, or she will find that she has married the American millionaire. And so the phantasy goes on. It starts in reality, but the Narcissistic temperament takes it right away from this. It must be nipped in the bud at the very beginning, if the habit of directive thought is to be established. As soon as the individual finds himself drifting in this way, wasting energy, fulfilling wishes by mere dreams, he must pull himself up short, and say to himself, "Here the real ends, there the phantasy begins. This is the point I must come back to, I must deal with this matter from the real point of view only, without allowing this phantasy to intrude itself."

And here again, much patience will be needed, for if the habit has already been cultivated, he will soon be back in phantasy again, probably in less than five minutes. But phantasy thought does not only mean day-dreams in the sense in which we have spoken of them here. It may take all sort of disguises, and what would be phantasy thought in one person, would be directive thought in another. In one case, the environment and education and inherent ability would not be of that order which could make the thoughts come to be facts; in the other case the abilities of the person might be sufficient to do so. Thus, were an ordinary person to sit in his arm-chair, and phantasy a wonderful plan for the conquest of Europe, without having either the will or the means of carrying out his ambition, that would constitute phantasy thinking pure and simple. If, however, a Napoleon did the same, with the will and the possible means, with the near aim at hand in the conquest of a small country, and the subsequent conquest of Europe as an ultimate one, his method of thought would have to be described as directive thinking. So that similar thinking in two different individuals may really be classified as two different principles of thinking.

I have no doubt that many readers will be saying to themselves now, "But my greatest pleasure is to be found in day-dreams. I find in directive thinking nothing but hard work."

In such a case, if the individual cannot enjoy his directive thinking, and he gets no emotional discharge by means of it, it is possible that his aims in life are unsuited to him, or that he has not sufficient aims in life, that his time is not as fully occupied with interesting *acts* as it should be. In such a case, subsidiary aims should be formed deliberately, wherein he could take an interest in directive thinking. *For it may be accepted as a fact that, with proper cultivation and education, more real pleasure can be found in suitable directive thinking than in any amount of day-dreams.* It is also a further fact that the individual's energy is not then wasted, but is more or less efficiently utilised. Moreover, instead of losing strength of character, he is now gaining it. Let it be borne in mind, always, that continual indulgence of phantasy thought, from its very ease, breeds the habit of inertia, for the individual's aims and wishes attain fulfilment without any need for activity on his part; and here a vicious circle is produced, because the inertia, which he has thus encouraged, now in its turn tends to make him resort to phantasy the more.

It is easy, of course, to say, "I will cut myself off from phantasy thought, I will pull myself up whenever this occurs, and leave it alone." But it is by no means easy to act up to this resolution. If, however, another kind of directive thought is deliberately substituted for the phantasy, the task is made very much easier. If the water in the bath is too hot, and we want it to cool rapidly, we do not merely turn off the hot tap, we simultaneously turn on the cold.

The task will be rendered more easy still, if the individual selects his subject of directive thought to replace phantasy beforehand, not waiting until the time comes. For instance, we will suppose that, as one subsidiary aim with which to fill in his time, a person has selected the collection of postage stamps. He will each day have in front of him some page which he wishes to arrange in chronological order, to consider from the point of view of water-marks and perforations; and he may make up his mind that as soon as he finds himself dealing in phantasy thought he will not only cut out the phantasy thought but will at once start arranging, in his mind, the stamps which he was shortly going to arrange in his book. It matters not in the least what form the substitute thought takes, so long as it possesses two qualities, (1) it is directive, *i.e.*, it is going to lead to some sort of actual change or action, and (2) that it bears a pleasurable interest. And for that reason, I have selected a very trivial form of directive thought as an example. The point is that the individual should select some subject in which he has a personal and active interest, as a subject with which he may replace phantasy thought, whenever the latter comes into his mind.

Phantasy thought may, further, not be of necessity thoughts impossible of fulfilment, except in the immediate present. Thoughts of erotic or other desires which intrude themselves at untimely moments, are phantasy thoughts, and some people frequently complain that they are annoyed by them, especially when they have no intention of actually fulfilling them in fact, or when the means of fulfilling them are not present. Here again, to have a subject ready at hand, or to have a substitute thought for the undesired thoughts is a very real assistance. Even a sentence thought out beforehand or a good maxim which can be repeated several times and considered, forms an excellent substitute thought with which to replace the unwanted phantasy.

Let us now consider a few other examples. The majority of educated people, of a so-called normal type, when they have completed their day's work, and are fatigued, require some sort of mental rest, and as a rule some kind of phantasy thought is resorted to in the evening. Also, when this fatigue is cumulative, they say, "We have worked eleven months, and now require one month's holiday." This is really an unconscious phantasy requiring a regressive reward. They are not really tired out, physically or mentally, but they have accumulated, after a series of postponements, a large number of Narcissistic efforts at phantasy; and the holiday which they now require is really to satisfy this. It is a return to childhood and the time of irresponsibility, and their occupations on the holiday may very likely be, to a large extent, similar to those with which they occupied themselves in childhood. They throw off their adult status and responsibility, and deliberately take this regressive reward. Even with normal people the idea of *rest* in the form of a holiday, often means nothing but phantasy thought, time disregarded, no effort of any sort to be made.

But in the less Narcissistic type of person who still retains directive thought even on a holiday—a holiday means merely change in immediate aim, change in occupation, rather than rest from aim and occupation.

Phantasy thinking may take many quite surreptitious forms. In old age, for instance, we know that type of person, who is quietly slipping into helpless imbecility. He is the same man, who, at an earlier age, lacked the habit of directive thought. On the other hand, there is our intellectual old man or woman, still full of the day's problems or politics, who indulged, in early life, but little in phantasies. Experience shows us that the influence of directive or undirective thought in youth may not only determine our happiness in declining years, but may even determine the actual age to which we live. For, paradoxically, it is the Narcissist, who of all people desires a long life, and who is, of all people, the least likely to attain old age. He frequently "worries himself into the grave."

We have not yet exhausted the forms of phantasy thought. A casual conversation between acquaintances in which no information of value is imparted, in which merely some emotional material is brought to the surface and thrown out, is undirective thought. The first person, interested in some emotional experience, recounts to the second the facts of that experience, often without arousing any emotional feeling in the second person. Such is the type of conversation which takes place over a vast majority of tea-tables. It is wasted energy.

Another example is that of conventional letter-writing, in certain cases. The duty letter which one person writes to another person is of the same type. The writer who deals with his or her experiences on a shopping expedition, who states a series of things which have happened, merely in order to enjoy them once again in phantasy, is performing the same waste of energy. There is no return for this expended energy, the rush of ideas produces no result. Perhaps the time is due for a letter to be written, and it is the turn of this person to write a letter. As a result of this conventional attitude, the writer has to resort to phantasy thought to satisfy the needs of the moment. We have pointed out that reading a novel is a form of phantasy thinking, in which we identify ourselves with the hero. The same occurs in our cinemas. Here, the pleasure of phantasy thinking is enhanced by the fact that the visual impression is produced direct, whereas in reading a novel the visual impression is by words only, and a certain amount of effort is needed to translate it in the mind into its pictorial form; and thus the cinematograph induces a form of phantasy thinking which needs the least effort of all to realise. It is within the reach of anyone possessing a few pence, and although the average person may regard it as educative and useful to the community, the magistrate who is dealing with the youthful delinquent knows the cinematograph to be very harmful to the child's mind. And there is no doubt that the unconscious effect of such mental stimuli is excessively deleterious to the race in general. The indulgence in it encourages the habit of phantasy thinking at a small cost, and such a habit soon becomes established as part of the individual's make-up. Nor does the evil stay itself here. For the phantasy in the cinematograph consists usually in the fulfilment of impossible wishes, and in this, as in other cases, the emotional output is increased out of all proportion to the real exciting causes. This results in a misplacement in the emotional output in the unconscious mind, which in its turn is the basis of many neurotic conditions which may even require a physician's aid to eradicate. And one must remember that a neurotic condition need not merely be the illness of an individual, it may be, and often is, the disease of a nation. Hence, like the fairy-tale, the cinema, as it is at present, should not be used as a child's pastime.

§2

In other forms of Narcissism also, we shall find it easier to break away from phantasy if we substitute a reality; that is, if we turn our flow of energy into a real, instead of an imaginary channel, instead of merely trying to dam the flow in the original channel. In cases where this Narcissism involves a bad habit, such as irritability, impatience, weeping, etc., the line that should be followed differs rather from that suggested in the case of day-dreams. In the first place, not only should we pull ourselves up short, but we should also bear in mind, immediately, the first part of the technique which we suggested in a previous chapter. That is to say, we should call to mind what our abnormal act really means, and having done this, having realised it in consciousness, *we should then endeavour to use the same energy which we should have used for this abnormal act in an immediate and useful manner*. Now, in all these cases, our abnormal reaction takes place because our omnipotence or sense of perfection is disturbed; and since this sense of perfection is not real, the easiest and most convenient channel for us to turn our energy into is one which still satisfies the sense of perfection, that is to say, one in which we may feel that *we are, by our act, becoming more perfect in reality, instead of clinging to our perfection in phantasy*. It is impossible to give examples to cover the very many reactions which may take place, but one actual example, given in detail, should be sufficient to enable the individual to invent others to suit his own case. Let us again take the case of the impatient man, in which the Time-factor has never been fully realised.

Let us say that he has entered a restaurant for lunch, and that having glanced down the menu, he then has to wait ten minutes before the waiter attends to him. Probably, after the first minute of that time, he has begun to get impatient; at the end of ten minutes he is either making up his mind to go without his lunch, so great is his irritability, or else he is, with great emotion, explaining to his neighbour how extremely inefficient this restaurant is, as regards management, service, and, in fact, everything connected with it. He is utterly unable to realise the facts of the case. Let us again refer to the facts for a moment. The restaurant is a business, and must make a profit; in order to do this, only a limited number of waiters can possibly be kept, and the number of these has to be regulated by the *average* number of customers, by the profit which it is possible to make in the neighbourhood, and other factors. In the second place, the luncheon hour is one at which the number of customers is well above the average, and therefore in which the service is bound to be the slowest; however good the management, however skilful the waiters, they are obliged to devote a certain number of minutes to each customer; and the probability is that our Narcissistic individual is being as well attended to as anybody else. He does not realise this however, he is not dealing with the facts at all. He merely knows that he wishes for an immediate meal, that his sense of perfection is thoroughly disturbed, and his unconscious idea is that if he is sufficiently impatient, what he wants will come to him immediately, just as it did in childhood.

Now let us see how he may deal with himself. We will suppose that he has read this chapter before his next visit to the restaurant in question. Once again he sits down, once again he finds he is kept waiting. His impatience begins to manifest itself in its early stages. He pulls himself up, and the first thing that he does is to realise the causes of his impatience, as set out in the last paragraph. He must go quickly over the original causes of his Narcissism in infancy, and of how he obtained means of satisfaction, and so developed his present habit of thought. He must run over the facts concerning the restaurant, and realise that it is a business place, and that it is at its busiest hour. In other words, he must get into full consciousness the various factors associated with this Narcissistic outburst of impatience. Then, let him realise as a kind of summary, "What I am actually objecting to is the disturbance of my unconscious feeling of omnipotence and perfection. Let me, however, turn this energy, utilise this time during which I am waiting in attaining a step nearer real perfection instead of bemoaning the loss of my imaginary perfection. Now, a step towards real perfection will be attained, if I overcome this habit of impatience. Let me, therefore, utilise this time in sitting here patiently, in worrying no longer about the time the waiter is taking, in being actually pleased with the fact that I am becoming more patient, and that my time is being usefully filled with a directive aim, which has as its object the same ultimate idea as the original phantastic one, namely, that of perfection."

Critics may here suggest that this long monologue on the part of the impatient individual might have been cut short by allowing him to say, "Obviously, the waiters are busy, it is no use being impatient, let me be patient." I must point out, however, that the result would probably not have been the same. The longer method has its value in the fact that he brings into consciousness the two ideas of perfection, the Narcissistic idea which is being hurt, and the real idea which he is desiring consciously to obtain. *And it is very much easier to turn energy from one channel to another, if there are lines of similarity between the two channels.*

Hence, when one's sense of perfection is assailed, let one turn one's energy into some form of thought which still satisfies the idea of perfection attained or attainable. A similar process can be gone through with any other Narcissistic form of trouble, and consists in recapitulating the causes, and in reaching a determined effort to deflect consciously the energy from the phantastic into the real. The same principle holds good for all temperamental troubles of this sort, but the individual will have to devise for himself a suitable formula to use to suit the needs of his own case.

Chapter 13. Auto-Suggestion

Suggestion, in one form or another, plays an extremely important part in the life of everyone. Suggestion consists in impressing upon the unconscious mind some idea or thought in such a way that the unconscious mind will take it and absorb it as part of itself, and utilise it unconsciously and instinctively. Quite unconsciously, throughout childhood and adult life, we are receiving suggestions from the actions of those around us.

For example, I remember as a boy going repeatedly with a relative to a friend's house. At the time, I did not notice that my relative invariably used the knocker, and never rang the bell, or rather I did not consciously notice it. On one occasion I, myself, was sent with a message to this house, and although I was in the habit of ringing bells whenever I went to other houses, at this particular one, I instinctively knocked only. The suggestion that I should knock upon that particular door had been implanted in me by the fact that I had repeatedly seen the same action take place, although I had paid no conscious attention to it. It had impressed itself upon my mind as the right action to take place, under the particular circumstances attending a visit to this house, so that I performed the action itself automatically, without any further thought in the matter.

The example impressed itself upon my mind, because while I was in the house, on this occasion, a man came to mend the bell, which had been out of order for many months. Hence, the reason my relative invariably knocked.

Suggestion of various kinds is a very powerful factor, and as in the example given above, it is for the most part an unconscious factor in determining our actions. But it is possible for us to give ourselves *conscious* suggestions which will afterwards cause us to act automatically, in accordance with the suggestion. A great deal too much, however, has been claimed for suggestion in recent months. There are many circumstances in which suggestion is not likely to be any good at all, there are also circumstances when it may arouse an actual opposition in the unconscious mind, where a counter-suggestion is set at work immediately, and the condition of the individual may actually be worse than before he started giving himself suggestions.

Apart from other things, one factor may be mentioned which is very antagonistic to suggestion, and that is *fear*, possibly fear which is for the most part unconscious. Thus, supposing that the alcoholic gives himself the suggestion that he shall pass a public-house without going into it, and he has a definite fear of the wish to go in; he will probably find that in suggesting that he shall not have the wish, he is actually re-enforcing the strength of the wish which is there. His unconscious counter-will is at work, and turning the force of the suggestion in the wrong direction, and he will very likely succumb to temptation more readily than before. Hence, in a subject where we have acute fear of failure, suggestion must be very carefully dealt with. Moreover, suggestion, to be efficient, must have other things in its favour, some knowledge, in fact, of the underlying causes of the deleterious action which we wish to eradicate. It is not impossible to improve oneself by suggestion, even though one may be ignorant of the cause of one's trouble, but I have found that it is infinitely more easy to obtain this improvement if one has previously brought into consciousness the underlying cause, and can therefore direct one's suggestion to this rather than merely to the effect or symptom. I have myself devised a method for the use of certain of my patients by means of which suggestion may be directed to both the cause and result, as indicated shortly. Ordinary methods of suggestion are frequently merely directed to the cure of the symptom rather than the disease; in fact, such auto-suggestion, popular as it has become, may frequently be likened to a doctor who treats small-pox by putting ointment on the spots, or appendicitis by giving morphia. It will be successful in those cases where the manifestations of the disease are worse than the disease itself; but when the causes are strong and virile, suggestion directed towards the symptom will not avail.

In an earlier chapter, we described how the individual suffering from deleterious abnormalities of temperament could, to some extent, trace the cause of this back to infancy. We told how this, in itself, would, if repeatedly brought to mind on succeeding occasions, produce considerable improvement. We have further discussed how he could consciously turn the energy from one form of reaction into another and more suitable form. All these methods, however, may be made considerably more efficient by the active use of auto-suggestion, as I have indicated, directed partially to the cause and partially to the result desired. Thus, the form which suggestion should take in the case of the man, whom we quoted in the last chapter as being over-impatient in the restaurant, would be somewhat as follows:

He would have to impress upon himself several suggestions; and in the case of each of these suggestions he would be required to form a mental picture of himself in the conditions to which the suggestions referred. Firstly, "In circumstances in which I have been accustomed to react with impatience, I will no longer act as I did when I was a little child." (In repeating this to himself in the manner to be referred to shortly, he should hold a picture of himself reacting impatiently when a child, and contrast it with the manner in which he ought to have acted.) Secondly, "Under conditions which have previously caused me to react with impatience, I will in future, at once think out the *real* circumstances of the case." (And another suitable mental picture should be visualised here, as also in each of the following suggestions.) Thirdly, "Under conditions which previously caused me to react with impatience, I will no longer be impatient." Fourthly, "Under conditions to which I have been accustomed to react with impatience, I shall now devote my energy to perfecting myself, in reality." Thus, he is taking himself through the stages from childhood onward, and re-educating himself in each stage by means of a forced education in which the individual "grows up" in reality from the point at which he stopped in childhood.

Not one, but all these thoughts, and possibly even intermediate ones that may develop, should be impressed upon the unconscious mind, so that they may act automatically. As to the method which should be adopted by the patient in giving himself suggestions, I recommend the following. That he first of all write down briefly the results of his self-examination, that he should take those results in chronological order, and write down from them suitable suggestions dealing with the various stages, such as I have just written with regard to the impatient man. That every night and morning, or at any other time during the day, he should for five or ten minutes lie down, relax himself, and close his eyes; that he should then repeat to himself fifteen or twenty times each of the suggestions, taking the earliest first, then the next, and so on. They need not be repeated out loud, but if repeated under the breath and accompanied by a suitable movement of the lips, it will suffice. Effort should be avoided; suggestion is not an effort of will so much as an impression effected by the imagination. When an individual is giving himself suggestion, he is not fighting an active battle, he is merely allowing ideas to sink into his mind; and if they are repeated often enough, like drops of water which in time wear a channel in the stone, they will make their mark and produce their effects in due course.

Suggestion, in fact, minimises the need for the use of will-power, at any given moment in a difficult situation. If the battle has been fought out beforehand in imagination, it will automatically succeed when the time comes. The will has played its part previously when adopting the method of suggestion.

This is not a text-book on suggestion, and I do not propose to go further into the method here. I merely wish to point out the practical efficiency of the use of a certain amount of auto-suggestion when applied in conjunction with the other methods of combating Narcissism already outlined, and when applied in an intelligent manner, so that not merely the symptoms, but the original causes themselves shall be affected by it.

Chapter 14. Conclusion

The previous portion of this book has been devoted to showing how Narcissism may be harmful, and how in its endeavour to obtain satisfaction it may render the individual unhappy in the utmost degree. It is possible that the reader will have gathered that the author regards Narcissism as wholly and completely a useless and detrimental element in life; the more so, since at various points we have had to emphasise that in one form or another very little of it persisting in adult life may be a great deal too much. It should be realised, however, that Narcissism to a slight extent, and at certain periods, plays an important and also necessary part in the individual's life. We mentioned at one place that a certain amount of identification was beneficial in choosing one's life partner. Whereas too much identification might lead to one's choosing a sexual partner of the same sex, a small amount of identification might lead to one's choosing a partner with the same tastes, and would further lead to a tendency to enjoy whatsoever the other one enjoyed, and to dislike what the other one disliked, and this similarity would lead to a certain harmony in life. *Narcissism is a normal thing in the new-born infant, and Narcissism is the root of many virtues; but its final adult form must be sublimated and very much attenuated.* It is like the salt in cooking; a little is essential to bring out the flavour, but a very little more spoils the whole dish.

A certain amount of self-love, self-appreciation, self-importance, and self-consciousness of one's own capacities is necessary in every one; without it he would be ill prepared to cope with men and circumstances. But this necessary self-importance and self-appreciation is not, as many might think, due to Narcissism alone. It has a slight Narcissistic element, but it is largely a resultant of other unconscious instincts, which we have not attempted to deal with here; and we only mention it, lest the reader should draw the conclusion that these necessary elements in our character are drawn purely from a Narcissistic basis, and that he should therefore be left puzzled as to how, if he should eradicate Narcissism, he would be able to retain necessary characteristics which apparently belong to this same instinct. It is also very necessary for the reader to bear in mind that much which may be developed from Narcissism is useful; even though the original from which it came may be dangerous and harmful. Moreover, a certain amount of enjoyment of phantasy such as is obtained from novels or theatres may be in many people quite a useful and adequate form of relaxation. With them it may be strictly cut off from real life, may be strictly limited as regards time and place, and, in fact, entirely under their control. In such persons it forms a useful element in their lives. I do not say that if their early education and environment had been different they might not possibly possess an even better form of recreation, but merely that, taking facts as they are, in certain cases it forms a useful factor in the working scheme of life.

In others, however, in those where it has exceeded the limits of absolute control, it is necessary, for the time being at least, to attempt to cut it out as completely as possible, because where it is allowed slight free play, it is liable to get out of hand, unless it can be dealt with absolutely at the will of the individual. Hence the necessity for such stringent treatment as I have laid down in the previous chapters of this book.

I have attempted to show that happiness is, for the most part, within the individual's own grasp. Happiness comes from within the individual and not from without. Unhappiness must not be confused with pain, either mental or physical, for pain is a normal reaction, to a harmful stimulus which all are liable to feel; it is for the most part beyond the individual's control so long as the stimulus persists; but the peace of mind, the absence of worry, of irritability, of perpetual uneasiness, which we call unhappiness, lies within the control of everybody. It largely consists in continually recognising what facts are unchangeable, and ceasing to bemoan or phantasy about these unchangeable facts. It is true that the road to happiness may be difficult if we have long been accustomed to tread the path of Narcissism, but it is equally true that if the advice laid down in this book be followed patiently and systematically, a very much happier frame of mind will be attained as a result. In a few cases, Narcissism is not a predominant factor causing the temperamental disturbance although superficially it may appear to be so. In such cases (where other primitive instincts are really of paramount importance) the same degree of improvement will not be attained by this method of self treatment and only a more prolonged course of regular psycho-analysis is likely to produce the desired result.

Happiness is not to be found by seeking happiness in the direct sense. This, I am aware, sounds very much like a mere high-sounding thought of a writer. It is the sort of phrase that people dismiss with the remark, "That is all very well in theory." This statement, however, is not made from any moral or sentimental point of view, nor on any purely theoretical grounds, but as a scientific fact, which has been demonstrated as the result of psychological research. It may be interesting to note here how much the psychology of happiness is in agreement with many of the teachings of the New Testament, although a different terminology and mode of expression may be used.

It was pointed out earlier how the individual who employed too much phantasy thought in youth might worry himself into an early grave, although he was the same individual who most desired a long life. It has now been shown that happiness does not come to those who seek happiness, but to those who can adapt themselves to realities, that is, to those who can control their Narcissism. Narcissism is not so very different from the word "self," as used in Christian teachings, and any who are interested enough to compare them will find that there is considerable parallelism between Christian teaching and certain psychological observations.

I must emphasise the fact once more that patience, that is a realization of the time factor, is very necessary for those who attempt self-treatment on the lines indicated in this book. For since lack of this is often one of their faults to start with, they may otherwise involve themselves in a vicious circle, from which they do not escape. Patience and attention to detail will, however, enable them to accomplish that improvement which they have set out to achieve. In the words of Horace, "Happiness is here, happiness is everywhere, if only a well-regulated mind does not fail you."

THE END